ORANGUTAN
Endangered Ape

ORANGUTAN
Endangered Ape

Text & Drawings by
ALINE AMON

ATHENEUM 1977 NEW YORK

FOR WILMA AND
CHARLES MUHLENBERG

Credits for illustrations and photographs appear on pages 162–163

Library of Congress Cataloging in Publication Data

Amon, Aline.
  Orangutan, endangered ape.

  Bibliography: p. 150
  SUMMARY: An account of one orangutan's life in the rain
forest is interwoven with both factual and mythical information
about these great apes which have become an endangered
species.
    1. Orangutan—Juvenile literature.   2. Rare animals—
Juvenile literature.   [1. Orangutan.
  2. Rare animals]   I. Title.
  QL737.P96A45   599'.884   76–41354
  ISBN 0–689–30563–X

Published simultaneously in Canada by
McClelland & Stewart, Ltd.
Manufactured by The Murray Printing Company
Forge Village, Massachusetts
Designed by Nora Sheehan
First Edition

Contents

Preface

Orangutan, Endangered Ape tells two stories. One describes the life of a wild orangutan, free in the forest. Alternate chapters follow the history of the apes and humans together—from early myths, through zoos and laboratories, to recent efforts at saving the threatened species.

In the end, however, both parts of the book recognize the impact of people on wildlife and wild places. Perhaps it really is a single story.

Acknowledgments

I AM GRATEFUL TO MRS. TOBY PYLE, OF THE
World Wildlife Fund's Washington office, for collecting material that might otherwise have not been available; Dr. Herman
Rijksen, for his approval of the project and his excellent
photographs; Dr. Duane M. Rumbaugh, for the scientific
papers on his research that he supplied; Mrs. Mary Griswold
Smith, of the National Geographic Society in Washington, for
her generous assistance in obtaining photographs; and many
others, both here and in England, who provided the names of
orangutans or other missing bits of information.

Dr. W. Amand, Curator of Mammals at the Philadelphia
Zoo, patiently answered my questions. Ann Hess, who has
raised some of the zoo's infant primates, introduced me to the
orangutans, told me their histories and shared her enthusiasm
for the apes.

I want particularly to thank Biruté Galdikas, who took time
out from her busy schedule during a brief visit to the United
States to read the manuscript and offer many helpful sugges-
tions, in telephone conversations and correspondence. Dr.
Jonathan Harrington, of the State University of New York
at Stony Brook, a primate biologist with field experience,
checked the book for accuracy. Both his scientific knowledge
and his sense of style proved invaluable. If any errors remain
in the text, it is the fault of the author.

The expert advice of my editor, Jean Karl, guided me in
smoothing rough passages and disentangling complicated ones
when I could no longer see the rain forest for the trees.

And finally, thanks to my family, who now know much more about orangutans than they ever thought possible: my husband, Larry, for his patience—and his proofreading; my son, Niel, for hours spent in the darkroom; and my daughter, Lauren, for permission to use her photograph as an example of one species of endangered primate.

ORANGUTAN
Endangered Ape

The Birth

GIBBERING, CHATTERING AND HOOTING filled the hot, damp air of the tropical rain forest, drowning the soft whimpers of an orangutan. Suddenly, she gave a short, sharp cry. It brought a surprised silence, soon broken by the clapping wings of a parrot. The brilliant bird darted away, frightened.

Voice by voice, the forest chorus began again. A large red ape, squatting in her leafy nest high in a tree, ignored the familiar sounds. She stared gravely at the small wet bundle in her hand. The baby had been born a minute before.

The mother gently cleaned its wrinkled face with her tongue and blew on its lips. The tiny fingers and toes

3

began to wiggle. As the ape licked the baby's damp, dark fur, its eyes opened and closed. It cried a little.

After a while, the mother bit through the umbilical cord. Then she relaxed in her nest. One hand held fast to a branch above her head and the other pressed the infant against her chest.

Birds and monkeys continued to call as they flew and foraged through the dense woods. A new orangutan had joined the jungle's inhabitants, but only her solitary mother cared.

Apes, People
& Ape People

ONCE UPON A TIME, TWO BIRDLIKE beings created all forms of life. One successful day, they made man and woman. Such an accomplishment demanded a celebration, and the creators feasted late into the night. The next day they were not feeling well. When they tried to make more of the wonderful humans, they forgot part of the recipe. They created orangutans instead.

According to this ancient Asian myth, the newborn orang and all her ancestors were only the results of a mistake.

Another old belief held that orangutans were people who had displeased the gods. In punishment the sinners were clothed in bright fur and sent to live in the high green world of the rain forest.

Other tales describe the animals as half ape and half person. The orangs were supposed to abduct human beings for their mates. The same story is told in Africa about chimpanzees and gorillas. It reveals less about the animals' appetites than it does about the imagination—and vanity— of people.

All these early myths and tales connect orangutans with people in one way or another. It is difficult to think about any animal except in human terms. A cuddly kitten is "cute as a baby."

It is even harder to watch any of the great apes without comparing their feelings and behavior to ours. Their expressive faces and useful hands, and their occasional efforts at walking on two legs, all mirror human ways too closely. It was natural for Asians and Africans, who lived close to the apes, to wonder where such creatures came from. How could they be related to people?

The Malaysians even name the red apes after themselves. On the islands, the animals are often called "Maias" or "Mawas," but everywhere they are known as orangutans. "Orang" means "person" or "reasonable being," while "utan" stands for "of the woods." For years the name has been translated "man of the woods," but the Malaysian language acknowledges that there are "reasonable beings" of both sexes. "Orang perempuan" is woman; "orang laki-laki," man.

There are rumors of other, even rarer, creatures in the

A drawing of the elusive Orang Pendek based on eyewitness reports.

rain forest, more truly half ape and half human than the orangutan. These hairy beings walk erect and come in a variety of sizes, called Orang Gandang (large person), Orang Letjo (gibbering person) and Orang Pendek (little person). Like their cousins in myth, or reality, the Abominable Snowman of the Himalayan mountains and the Bigfoot of the American Northwest, these human orangs are seldom seen and never captured.

Like the other ape people, however, they have left footprints. Dr. John MacKinnon, a British scientist who spent many months in Borneo studying wild orangutans, once discovered two dozen strange footprints. They seemed almost human except that the largest toes were on the outside. Bears also have long outer toes, but these prints were too large for the only species in the rain forest, the sun bear. And there were no claw marks.

Although MacKinnon was puzzled, his native helpers were not. They identified the maker of the prints as "Batutut," a shy, four-foot, upright creature with a long black mane.

Later Dr. MacKinnon saw casts of similar footprints in a Malaysian museum, prints thought to belong to the Orang Pendek. In Sumatra, the Orang Pendek and Batutut are called the Sedapa. Whatever its name, something unknown but quite human is believed to live in the forests.

It is always possible that the mysterious prints were made by a new species of bear. The rain forests shelter an unbelievable variety of life. There are more than fifteen hundred species of vertebrates, including at least three hundred mammals, in southeastern Asia. The islands of

Footprints attributed to Orang Pendeks and those of an orangutan. The shaded prints of a mother and child show the narrow heel noticed by MacKinnon, and the dotted print has a heavy outer toe. The orangutan's prints differ from the other primate ones because it walks on the sides of its curled feet. These "hooks" are better adapted to aerial travel than to the flat ground.

Borneo and Sumatra, where the orangutans live, have three thousand species of large trees. An unimaginable number of insects crawl, hop and fly through every level of the woods.

Scientists have just begun to study small areas of this teeming world. New forms of life might still be hidden in the almost impenetrable forest. In 1975, two unknown animals were discovered: a pouched mouse in Australia and a South American wild pig that was thought to have become extinct ten thousand years ago. Perhaps the next new creature will be found in the Asian wilderness. Will it be a different bear—or the red ape's cousin, Orang Pendek?

The Baby

AS THE FUR OF THE NEWBORN MAWA dried, it brightened in color. The four-pound infant made an orange splash against the darker chestnut coat of her mother, over twenty times heavier than the baby.

Mawa's little orangutan face was startlingly human. She had a high, round forehead without the heavy brow ridges of the other apes, gorillas and chimpanzees. Her small, neat ears were much like ours. Her brown-skinned face was bare, rough and goose-pimpled. Light areas around her big bright eyes and mobile mouth emphasized her expression. Her mother had lost the light patches as she grew. Her blue-gray face seemed melancholy. But Mawa's, framed in a halo of long copper wisps, was alert and merry.

After the baby's birth, her mother, Uta, did not wander far. When she was not feeding, she rested in a nest with little Mawa held to her chest.

Mawa clung to her mother instinctively, her small fingers and toes entangled in the long fur. Still, at first, Uta held her baby firmly while she travelled with the usual orangutan caution. She never released one branch to reach for another unless she was securely balanced. Her long curved fingers and toes turned her hands and feet into hooks made for gripping branches. Her thumbs and big toes were too small to get in the way. Uta was even missing the nail of one useless big toe and the whole last joint of the other, like many orangutans.

Uta began to exercise Mawa's little arms and legs while they rested. She pushed and pulled the scrawny limbs and encouraged her to crawl around the nest. Sometimes Uta placed the infant on her head, where Mawa clung like a round-bellied, skinny-legged spider.

Soon Mawa could hold onto her mother safely. Then, when Uta was ready to travel, she shifted the infant from her front to her side. She could move more easily with Mawa hanging on behind her arm, though she still proceeded carefully, grasping tightly with three of her hooks while the fourth reached for a new hold.

After Uta had eaten the last of the food near Mawa's birthplace, she wandered in search of more nourishment along stream banks, mountain ridges and other natural features of the land. The forests were less fruitful from mid-December to mid-June than they would be later in the year. Now, in April, only a few fruits were ready to be picked.

Once Uta clambered into a mass of vines, seeking both the tender pulp beneath the bark and new leaves unfolding in the sun. Another ape joined her. Mawa peered out from under her mother's arm. The cinnamon-colored visitor seemed large to the baby, but he was only half the size of Uta. Mawa kept peeking at the newcomer, but her mother ignored him. Although he seemed very busy browsing, he stole a glance at the pair from time to time.

As the light faded toward evening, Uta climbed to a nearby tree already thick with small soft leaves. She stopped at a level place where several sturdy branches joined sixty feet up in the air. Still holding safely to a branch overhead with one arm, the ape used the other to sweep and bend branches toward herself, folding them underfoot.

When she had made a stout platform, Uta sat down on it and spun slowly in a circle. Here and there she added a twig to a weak spot, patting it into place with her fist. Finally, pinching stems between her fingers, she pulled off handfuls of leaves to cushion the nest. Then she curled up with Mawa for the night.

Suddenly the afternoon visitor swung into the nest. Uta repulsed him quickly with an angry snarl, but he did not go far. Leaves drifted down on mother and daughter. The young ape was making his nest just a little higher in the same tree.

Mawa did not notice. She was drinking deeply the milk

that would be her main nourishment for at least a year. She did not know that the other youngster, Tan, wanted to suckle, too. She did not know that he was her brother. But Tan recognized the mother he had left so recently. He was jealous, like a human child.

Shrinking Apes

ORANGUTANS AND THE HUMANS THEY
resemble have known each other for at least
thirty-five thousand years. At Niah, on the northwestern
coast of Borneo, there is a large network of caves. They
were used as homes and burial grounds during the early
Stone Age, before the primitive people bravely moved out
into the forests to live.

Archeologists digging carefully through centuries of
debris on the twenty-seven-acre floor of the Great Cave of
Niah found a human skull thirty-five to thirty-eight thousand years old. Among the bones of early people were those
of other primates, monkeys and orangutans. Perhaps the
apes were kept as half-tame pets. It is certain that they were

used for food. Some of their bones were charred by fire.

Primates made up half of the Stone Age diet, with orangutans a favorite meal. The only more popular food was wild pig. The menu included bats, birds, rats, lizards, turtles, fish, tapir, rhinoceros, wild ox and bear.

The prehistoric orangutans lived on the Asian mainland further north than the apes of today. Then the climate of southern China was wet and warm. These apes were immense. Huge teeth from the creatures, dating from the early Pleistocene epoch two or three million years ago, have been found in Chinese apothecary shops. They were sold as "dragons' teeth," full of powers both medicinal and magical.

During the Pleistocene, repeated ice ages chilled the earth. As drying winds blew and the air grew cold, the apes wandered south to warmer climates near the equator.

While much of the world's water was locked into ice, the seas shrank. Land bridges connected the Asian islands with mainland China. The early orangs and other tropical wildlife crossed them in the search for warmth.

When the earth entered an interglacial period, some of the ice melted and filled the seas. As the waters rose, orangutans were cut off from their ancestral environment, marooned on the islands of Borneo, Sumatra and Java.

By the early Holocene, or modern, epoch, perhaps twenty thousand years ago, the apes were extinct in Java. They had shared that island with *Homo erectus*, an early form of human being. This apelike creature was a more successful primate than its red-haired cousin and might

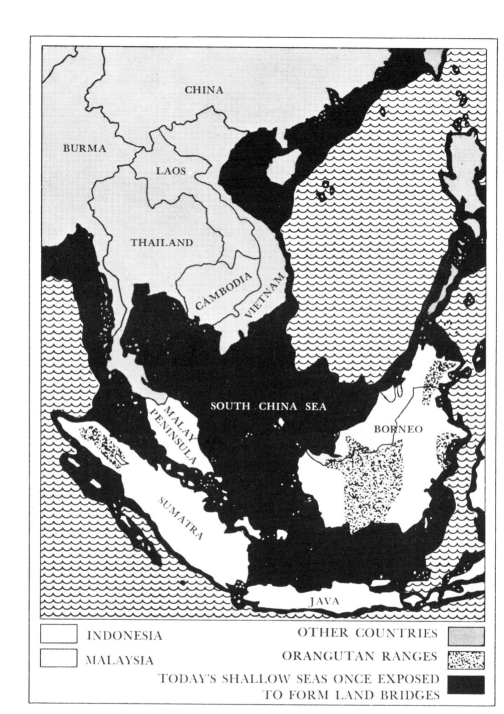

INDONESIA		OTHER COUNTRIES	
MALAYSIA		ORANGUTAN RANGES	

TODAY'S SHALLOW SEAS ONCE EXPOSED
TO FORM LAND BRIDGES

have caused the extermination of the orangutan. The animals could have been killed because they dared to eat the fruits of the forest needed by people, as well as for food.

The extinct Javanese orangutans were larger than the present-day ones but already much smaller than the ancient apes. The dragons' teeth suggest that those beasts were forty percent bigger than their descendants today. Such heavy animals might have lived like gorillas, travelling and feeding on the ground, with a large male to lead and protect the group.

This way of life could explain why the male orangutans are still bigger than the females, even though they now stay in trees much of the time. Most arboreal, or tree-living, primates show little difference in size between the sexes. But an impressive male is an advantage to ground-dwelling species. The male orangutan, like the male gorilla, can become twice as heavy as the female.

Generation after generation, orangutans grew smaller during the long years of their island life. In the tropical rain forests, travel is difficult on the swampy ground. It is easier to follow the aerial highways made by the interlacing branches of trees. And the fruit and leaves the orangutans eat are up in the forest canopy.

The smaller apes could move further through the tangled greenery on narrow branches. Adapting to the new environment, the giant dragons evolved over hundreds and thousands of years into the orangs of today.

Even now the orangutans still deserve the name "great apes." They are unable to swing through the trees with

Homo Erectus on Java teasing a giant tortoise. The greater intelligence and abilities of these primates threatened the orangutans and other animals of that island.

the speed of gibbons, the lesser apes. Fully grown males can reach two hundred fifty pounds. Perhaps this size helps them attract the attention of the smaller females. It has not protected them from their only dangerous predators, the people who have shared their islands, from *Homo erectus* to *Homo sapiens*.

The Forest

MAWA LIVED IN A THREE-STORIED HOME.
The crowns of the largest trees made up the top story, with
towering two hundred fifty foot tapangs the tallest of all.

The broad crowns of these trees gather in much of the
sun that falls on the forest. The rest of the light is absorbed
by the continuous canopy of treetops below the scattered
giants. This second story of dense foliage runs from about
twenty to seventy feet high. Ropes of woody lianas knit
branches together or hang in twisted snarls. Ferns, fungi
and flowers burst from cracks and crannies in the trees
where they are rooted. These epiphytic plants can live far
above the earth by absorbing the rains that fall on them.

Through this green world run aerial highways for every
species, from ants to orangutans. Monkeys swing from

branch to liana to branch, while birds zigzag deftly among the leaves.

Other flyers glide through the forest, unusual ones adapted to their life aloft. A tree snake, ribs flattened to broaden its slim form, slips through the air. A foot-long lizard, the draco, has five or six pairs of ribs extending from its body and covered with brightly colored skin. It resembles a giant butterfly when these ribs are opened, fan-like, for flight. Even frogs take to the air, thrusting out big webbed feet to brake their descent like four parachutes.

Mammals also adapt to life in the forest canopy. Flying squirrels reach vast sizes. The colugo, an odd animal related to no other one, is a greenish-gray beast the size of a cat. It has membranes stretching from head to legs to tail tip. When they are spread, the colugo becomes an animated kite able to glide more than one hundred and fifty yards.

All the animals in the high treetops must be agile and able to survive in their windy world. Strong hands clutch branches. Sharp claws slice securely into bark. One primitive primate, the saucer-eyed, nocturnal tarsier, has long legs for grasshopper leaps. Pads on its feet hold it wherever it lands, even on steep, slick surfaces.

In the upper stories of the rain forest, sunshine and breezes dry and warm the air during the day. But the lowest story, up to twenty feet or so, stays constantly dim and damp without wind or sun to change the climate. Worms and amphibians, nocturnal anywhere else, come out during the day. Their thin skins are protected by the shade and moisture of the forest floor.

Where the tree cover is complete, little undergrowth can survive in the perpetual shade of the lower story. But if even a fallen branch lets some light filter through, bushes, shrubs, palms and vines fight for space with saplings that are trying to force their way into the canopy.

The rich green of the woods is brightened by flowers most of the year. On the ground, sucking nourishment from vines, blooms the giant parasite, Rafflesia, more than two feet across. Its five tough petals, spotted red and white and brown, circle a foot-deep, rotten-smelling cup. Farther up sprays of tiny orchids sparkle against the brown bark of the trees where they hang. Across the high canopy, pink and white masses of blossoms float on a sea of green. One kind of tree blooms constantly for a hundred years. But some times are more flower-filled than others. Then the dark earth becomes a mosaic of fallen white and rose and yellow petals.

In our forests, a grove of birch may border a stand of pine. In Borneo, individuals of a species stand alone, surrounded by other types of trees. Orangutans must search far for their favorite foods. Trees of the same kind not only grow by themselves, they follow different schedules for fruit and flower. Some species only bear every five years, while others fruit almost monthly.

To thrive on such erratic sources of food, an orangutan must know its part of the forest well and remember the spacing and timing of the harvests.

Uta had been forming mental maps for over twenty years. Still, the first year of Mawa's life was a hard one.

Strong storms had torn blossoms from many trees and killed the bees that would have pollinated them. Fruit was scarce, and Uta had to travel farther to eat less than ever before in her life.

Satyrs &
Pygmies

L ONG BEFORE ANY EUROPEAN HAD
seen a great ape, travellers and traders
brought tales of them from Africa and Asia. With only
these fanciful stories as guides, people developed strange
ideas. Perhaps the myths of half-human, half-animal creatures grew from these rumors. The earliest Gorgons had
apelike faces surrounded by hair, curly hair that later
turned into writhing serpents.

In the first century, Pliny the Elder, a Roman of great
curiosity and learning, wrote about a number of unusual
human races. One kind had a single foot and another just
one eye.

Pliny described the "satyrs" of India as the swiftest of

creatures, sometimes running on four legs, sometimes on two. Could they have been gibbons? These small apes walk erect more often than the larger ones. A mountain tribe, with furry clothing and dog-shaped heads, barked instead of speaking. Baboons, apes or imagination?

Real knowledge about the great apes did not reach Europe until the sixteenth century. Then explorers from Portugal, Spain, England and the Netherlands began to roam widely over the seas. They set up trading posts on the African coast and the shores of Asia. And the apes arrived in Europe.

Specimens of the animals came singly and slowly at first. No one could get an overall picture of the members of the ape family and their relationship to each other. One misconception followed another.

The first complete and careful description of an ape was written by a famous Dutch doctor, Nicolass Tulp, in 1641. The ruler of the Netherlands, Frederick Henry, Prince of Orange, kept this animal in his private menagerie. Tulp named it *Satyrus indicus,* after Pliny's Indian satyr, but explained that it was also called "orang-outang" because of its human face.

Oddly, Tulp's ape was not an Asian orangutan at all but an African chimpanzee. It was probably a pygmy chimp, since it had webbing between its second and third toes.

In 1658 Jacob Bontius, also Dutch, made what is considered the first reference in scientific literature to the orangutan. But his description does not seem very scientific today.

"Yet regard this wonderful monster with a human face . . . walking erect, first that young female satyr . . . hiding . . . her face with her hands . . . weeping copiously, uttering groans, and expressing other human acts so that you would say nothing human was lacking in her but speech. The (Asians) say, in truth, that they can talk, but do not wish to, lest they should be compelled to labor . . . The name they give to it is Ourang outang."

A Dutch woodcut of 1669 shows some unusual orangutans. The strange figure on the right must have been the ideal orang for artists of the time. Creatures with the same smile and tapering toes illustrated works by both Tulp and Beeckman.

Halfway around the world, Africans held a similar belief about chimpanzees—they avoid speech just to escape
from working. Bontius was scornful of the idea, though, as
he was of the theory that orangutans were the offspring of
humans and apes. Such stories, he wrote, could only be
believed by boys who had not yet begun to shave.

Forty years later the first living ape to reach England
arrived—and died. A Dr. Edward Tyson dissected the infant animal with great care. Comparing its anatomy to
other primates, he found forty-seven features resembling
human ones and thirty-four closer to monkeys. Tyson decided the ape was "an intermediate link" between monkeys
and people in "the chain of creation."

Tyson's studies of his "Orang
Outang" prove that it was a
chimp.

Dr. Tyson described his findings in a book published in 1699, *Orang-outang . . . or the Anatomy of a Pygmie compared with that of a Monkey, an Ape, and a Man.* But his orang-utang, too, was a chimpanzee.

Tyson left "satyr" out of his chimp's several names, since he believed that those Indian animals were probably a kind of monkey. But he added "pygmie." There had been rumors of midget peoples since the fourth century B.C., but no pygmies had been discovered. Tyson decided that the human appearance and small size of his ape (an infant chimpanzee) and Tulp's (a grown pygmy chimp) made them the source of the stories about little people.

The Acrobat

THE SCARCE AMOUNT OF FRUIT DUR-
ing her first year did not affect little Mawa. Uta's milk
remained sufficient, and the baby gained a pound each
month.

By the time Mawa was one, she had all her baby teeth.
She had already begun to sample tidbits of food Uta spilled
on her fur. After a year of almost permanent body contact
with her mother, the small ape became more adventurous.
Curiosity called her further from Uta, but not too far. She
could always hurry back to a safe nest in the long chestnut
fur.

During her second year, Mawa proved herself an ac-
complished acrobat. Like all orangutans, she had extremely

28

THE ACROBAT | 29

flexible joints and lacked a certain ligament, the *ligamentum teres,* which ties the thigh to the hip. Without it, she moved her legs as freely and widely as her arms. Mawa could even scratch her back with her toes.

With an agility Uta no longer knew, the light little ape swung gaily through the trees while her mother squatted on the heavier branches. Orangutans do not have our well-muscled seats or the padded bottoms of some monkeys and prefer to crouch on their heels rather than sit on hard surfaces.

For the first year, Uta had been Mawa's only playmate, tickling or nibbling the infant gently. But the grave adult was seldom playful. Oddly, she did romp occasionally with Tan, who stayed near his family for several months. More often, though, Uta was so nasty to her son that he sometimes squeaked in fear if she just looked at him. This strange mixture of behavior had its effect. Tan became increasingly independent and spent fewer and fewer days with his mother.

Once, when he was back with his family, an adolescent male orangutan with a younger juvenile companion came to the tree where Uta and her children were feeding. Tan became part of the roughhouse fun and followed the two youngsters when they wandered away. He never returned.

Bright blossoms burst out after the lean year, promising rich harvests later, but fruit was still scarce. Uta ate leaves and ferns and tender new shoots just beginning to unfold. If she found a nest of tree-living termites, she scooped up the tasty insects, adding protein to her diet.

One day a gibbon family paused near the pair of orangutans. A skinny little one crept close to Mawa and poked her. It was an invitation to play. Adept as the baby orang had become, she was no match for the agile gibbon. Mawa declined the invitation by fleeing to her mother for comfort.

Mawa could play happily by herself for hours with only toys from the trees. She tossed leaves about and beat herself softly on her head and back with twigs. She swung rhythmically back and forth, dangling from a tough vine she had looped over a branch. She was an orangutan, a solitary ape.

As Uta and Mawa wandered through the forest, they often heard the distant calling of the least social of the orangutans, the adult males. One time a giant tree fell, its shallow roots unable to hold it against the powerful leverage of a windstorm. The crash was answered by a call from a much closer male. A bubbling noise rose to one roar and then another and another. The sound tapered off to deep groans and mumbling and muttering, like a passing storm.

Uta scooped up Mawa and moved away from the call as swiftly as she could. With a dependent baby, she had no time for romance.

The two reached the place where the fallen tree had torn a gap in the canopy. Uta began to rock, sending their tree swaying in wider and wider arcs. As it bent across the empty place, the ape reached out and caught a branch on the other side of the gap. Mawa climbed up on her mother's back and along her arms, crossing to the further trees on a living, furry bridge.

Then Uta swung over to her daughter and immediately began searching for soft leaves or sweet buds, the call of the nearby male forgotten. She had successfully escaped him, warned by his loud objections to the crashing tree.

Jocko & Pongo

D ANIEL BEECKMAN DESCRIBED A real orangutan, not a chimp or satyr or pygmy, in a 1714 book, *A Voyage to and from the Island of Borneo*. Beeckman, a ship's captain, was the first Englishman to visit orangutan territory. He wrote, "The Monkeys, Apes, and Baboons are of many different Shapes and Sorts; but the most remarkable are those they call Oran-ootans . . . these grow up to be six Foot high; they walk upright, have longer Arms than Men, tolerable good Faces . . . no Tails nor Hair, but on those Parts where it grows on human Bodies; they are very nimble footed and mighty strong; they throw great Stones . . . (and) Sticks at those Persons that offend them."

Beeckman kept a baby orang for seven months until it died of the "Flux." He thought his pet a "great Thief" with a love for alcohol. When no one was looking, the ape scooted to the punch bowl or stole a bottle of brandy, drank deeply, and then carefully replaced the bottle.

In 1707 two men were born who would become famous for the many-volumed natural histories they wrote. One was a Frenchman, George-Louis Leclerc, Comte de Buffon, and the other was the Swedish Carl Linnaeus.

Linnaeus originated the system of identifying plants and animals with two names, one for the genus and one for the species, a method of classification still followed by scientists today.

The resemblance of the ourang outang described by Bontius to a human being caused Linnaeus to include that ape in the genus *Homo,* as *Homo troglodytes,* or "cave-dwelling man," a strange name for an arboreal ape. Equally strange were Linnaeus's descriptions of its crinkly white hair and hissing voice. He also mentioned "travellers' stories" about the orangs' belief that the world was made just for them. At some future time, they will rule it again.

The Comte de Buffon recognized only one species of ape but he divided these animals into two groups by size. The small ones, including Tulp's satyr and Tyson's pygmy, were "Jockos." Gorillas were still unknown, but if the tales of big African apes were true, they would be "Pongos," like the large orangutans.

Buffon found a moral in the orangutan's resemblance to humans. "This Orang-outang or Pongo is only a brute, but a brute of a kind so singular, that man cannot behold it without contemplating himself, and without being thoroughly convinced that his body is not the most essential part of his nature."

In 1776 a live orangutan was sent to another Prince of Orange, William V. She was studied by the director of the Prince's zoo, Arnout Vosmaer, in his home before public demand forced him to display her in the menagerie. This exotic import was chestnut colored and "of a melancholy appearance." She was not fierce, as expected, but fond of company. Sometimes she took hay from her bed, made it into a comfortable heap and motioned to her keeper that he should sit next to her.

This ape shared a taste for alcohol with Beeckman's baby orang. Once she escaped and "during its state of liberty, it had, among other things, taken the cork from a bottle of Malaga wine, which it had drunk to the last drop, and had set the bottle in its place again. When presented with strawberries on a plate, of which it was extremely fond, it was very amusing to see it take them up one by one with a fork and put them in its mouth. . . . After eating, it always wiped its mouth, and when presented with a toothpick, used it in a proper manner."

This polite primate died after seven months.

At the time all imported apes had been females or young. It was Vosmaer, again, who received the first adult male orangutan for dissection. This Pongo had been shot in the far East and shipped preserved "in liquor."

The trade in orangutans between the Netherlands and

An artist's idea of how Vosmaer's "Pongo" must have looked while it was alive.

the Dutch East Indies had become brisk. The apes were appropriate gifts for the Princes of Orange from their far-away colonies, and the seamen found them amusing companions during the long voyages home.

The transplanted apes died promptly. Still another Dutchman, Pieter Camper, obtained a number of their bodies for dissection and study. At the time people believed that there were two orangutans, a red one from Asia and a black one from Africa (the chimpanzee), but Camper denied this. He felt his specimens were too different from Tyson's pygmy. Toward the end of the eighteenth century his work finally put the orangutan in a separate species.

But even after the middle of the nineteenth century

This illustration from the 1830's shows both the "red" and the "black" orangutans.

when the orangutans gained a genus of their own, some confusion remained. The appealing babies looked so little like the frightening males that there were thought to be two, or even three, species of orangutan. Even today the people of Borneo use the name "Mawas kesa" for small apes, "Mawas rambai" for medium-sized ones and "Mawas timbau" for the largest.

The infant orang has the most vertical face of all the apes, with a small round snout set below a high forehead. As it grows, its forehead recedes while its snout protrudes.

A late nineteenth century book, published after it was known that there was only one orangutan, suggested that this facial change might explain a difference in the temper, as well as the appearance, of the young and old.

"The general impression at present is, that the docility and gentleness of the young becomes changed into ungovernable ferocity. . . . How far this corresponds with the recessions of the foreheads of the adult skulls, it would be interesting to trace."

The Day
& the Night

AS THE GROWING LIGHT WASHED THE
shadows from the sky, Mawa woke to the hoots and whistles
of a nearby gibbon. Soon his mate joined the song to the
new day and then their young.

After the sun burned away the mist, Uta sat up, yawning. She scratched her belly and stretched her long arms
to loosen the muscles. It was time to start the day's serious
business of foraging.

At midmorning the long call of a male orang sounded
from the distance. An even further call answered it and
then another. The ritual of announcing where they were
completed, the males fell silent.

The gibbons continued their choruses as they swung

and cartwheeled through the territories they claimed. A woodpecker drummed. Heavy-headed hornbills squawked, and lesser birds chattered and sang. As the air warmed, cicadas joined the cacophony, their metallic buzzes rising and falling in rhythm.

There had been no rain the day before. June was in the dry season when only half as much rain fell as during the wet season. The day grew hotter, and Uta ended her foraging earlier than usual. After pulling a nest together quickly, she spent a few more minutes gathering fruit for a bedtime snack. Throughout the baking noon hours, the apes slept.

After their long nap, Uta and Mawa climbed through the forest canopy searching for more fruit. The older ape stopped at a hole in a tree trunk and thrust her fist in it. Water gathered there clung to her fur. She licked the glistening drops thirstily, while Mawa watched and learned.

Drongos, black birds with swallow tails, also explored the forest. Their loud calls attracted a flying, flitting, hopping parade of other birds—warblers, white eyes, flycatchers, babblers, even the bigger jays and magpies. As the troop made its way noisily through the woods, the birds shook leaves, bent twigs and scratched the earth. Clouds of insects rose in frightened flight. Others scurried away, but did not go far. Their winged tormentors promptly gobbled them up. Small furry beasts followed the flock, and even a snake attended the feast.

As dusk came, the two apes were still eating, making up

for time lost during their long nap. Satisfied munching could be heard in the sudden quiet of the darkening forest.

Then the tree frogs began to peep, joined by the tinny wails of bush crickets.

Cheeping, jostling bats had hung upside down all day, clustered in dead trees. Now they dropped and then rose on five-foot-wide wings. They soared off to find the fruit that nourished them as well as the orangutans.

Night came quickly as blackness oozed up from the forest floor into the canopy. Near the top, silver coins of moonlight slipped through the cover. They danced on the leaves, shedding a flickering reflection on Uta's gentle face.

As the song of the bush crickets died down, the ground crickets came out of their nests, buzzing. Night birds circled overhead, crying while they hunted. A deer barked, and an owl answered with its echoing hoot.

Tiny mouse deer, less than a foot tall, trod daintily on the forest floor. One stopped under the orangutans' tree to nibble the fruit they had dropped.

A large, slow shrew with a naked tail slunk across the ground searching for worms. Although the moonrat's white coat was visible in the dark, he was not afraid of any other animal. His foul smell protected him from predators.

Small lights speckled the black earth. Rotting leaves were laced with fine networks of luminous mold. Mushrooms glowed gold or green. Bright dots moved slowly in the dark, shining from the backs of crawling glowworms.

The trees also twinkled with the sparkle of fireflies. The males were sending their silent messages of light to any females who might be near.

Uta and Mawa retired, bellies full from their late snacks. Only an occasional grunt came from their nest. The fruit tree was taken over by the giant bats, still quarrelling as they ate.

Orangutan Tales

THE GREATER THE NUMBER OF orangutans in Europe, the more people were fascinated by these near relatives. It seemed as if anyone who had seen one of the apes had to tell its story.

A renowned French naturalist, Georges Léopold Nicolas Frédéric, Baron de Cuvier, was primarily interested in fossils and the anatomy needed to identify them. He studied the orangutans' structure seriously, but left his concern with stones and bones long enough to write about the apes' abilities, too. "They drink from a glass, eat with a fork or spoon, make use of a dinner-napkin, wait at table behind their master's chair like a servant, and, it is said, can assist him to wine."

42

One orang Cuvier watched was given to Empress Josephine of France in 1808. The ape became fond of two kittens, which she liked to put on her head. The small cats were not happy with this arrangement and dug their claws in deeply for fear of falling. The uncomfortable orangutan then tried repeatedly to pull out their claws, without success. She must have decided the pleasures of having a cat on her head outweighed the resulting scratches, however, and she continued to wear her unusual headpiece during her short life.

Ten years later, a Dr. Clarke Abel sailed to England with his pet Pongo. His long story of the voyage gave the fullest account yet of orangutan antics.

The ape had been allowed his freedom on land and cleverly defeated attempts to cage or chain him. After proving his success as an escape artist, the orangutan was allowed to roam the ship.

All orangutans, from Empress Josephine's to the present day zoo inhabitants, enjoy putting things on their heads. Without a kitten to wear as a hat, this ape makes do with straw.

Playing tag with the sailors, he soon proved himself the ablest acrobat. The orang would begin a game by giving a sailor a playful push. Then he would race up into the rigging. If he could not avoid his pursuer by sheer speed, he would swing out of reach on a rope. Other times he waited, motionless, tempting a sailor to come close. At the last moment, the clever ape slid quickly down the nearest rope to the deck.

Sometimes he let himself be caught. Then there would be a mock wrestling match in which neither man nor ape was hurt.

The orangutan claimed the sails folded at the foot of the main mast as his nest but he allowed Abel to share the niche, where the doctor also liked to rest and read.

When all the ship's sails were set, the orangutan's bedding was high in the shrouds. Then he tumbled blankets out of the sailors' hammocks or stole clothing they had hung up to dry.

Food was even more important to this ape than his sleeping quarters. Abel always carried fruit or "sweetmeats." As soon as the doctor came on deck, the orangutan picked his pockets. Sometimes Abel ran away to tease his pet, but the ape followed him through the rigging and across the decks until he caught his tempter and frisked him for treats.

When repeatedly shown an orange he was not allowed to take, the orangutan threw a temper tantrum, rolling and screaming on the deck. On several occasions after he was refused the fruit, the ape threw himself over the side of the ship.

The first time Abel thought that the frustrated beast had committed suicide. Then he found his pet hidden in the chains hanging from the side of the boat.

The ape understood what might happen if he really went overboard. He once tried to toss a cage of three monkeys into the sea. Food was the motive again. The monkeys had some in their cage they would not share with their large and jealous relative.

Not all the sailors were friendly. Some people seem to be unable to leave a lower primate in peace. The orangutan showed remarkable patience with his tormentors. Abel noticed that "his mildness was evinced by his forebearance under injuries, which were grievous before he was excited to revenge; but he always avoided those who often teased him."

One of the orangutan's favorites was the boatswain, who shared his meals with the ape—when the hungry creature had not already stolen the biscuits and grog. The boatswain taught him to use a spoon and he "might be often seen sitting by his cabin-door enjoying his coffee . . . with a grotesque and sober air that seemed a burlesque on human nature."

In London at last, Abel continued to observe this orangutan. The doctor was disappointed. The animal failed to learn more than two new tricks. He was trained to kiss his keeper and to walk on two legs, but not easily. Abel explained, "So difficult is it indeed for him to keep the upright position for a few seconds . . . that he is obliged, in the performance of his task, to raise his arms above his head, and throw them behind him to keep his balance

The orangutan described by Menault aping his elderly visitor.

. . . a well-trained dancing dog would far surpass him in the imitation of the human posture."

An apparently more talented orangutan was described by a Frenchman, Ernest Menault, who visited the ape "accompanied by an illustrious old gentleman, who was a clever, shrewd observer. His somewhat peculiar costume, bent body, and slow, feeble walk at once attracted the attention of the young animal, who . . . kept his eyes fixed on the object of his curiosity. We were about leaving, when he approached his new visitor, and, with mingled gentleness and mischief, took the stick which he carried, and pretending to lean upon it, rounding his shoulders, and slackening his pace, walked round the room, imitating the figure and gait of my old friend. He then gave him back the stick of his own accord, and we took our leave, convinced that he also knew how to observe."

The Orphan

THE FOREST GAVE THE ORANGUTANS
unending varieties of fruit—pods plump with seeds, purple
mangosteens, juicy plums, rambutans. In the abundance
of August, ninety percent of Uta's food could be her fa-
vored fruits.

Best of all were the heavy oval durians. Malaysians also
prized the football-sized fruit and its seeds, which they
roasted and ground into flour, but orangutans had first
chance at the crop. They liked the durians even before they
ripened.

Uta supported a prickly fruit with one hand while she
tore it from the tree with the other. Although humans
have to use machetes to crack the thick rind, she ripped it

47

open with her strong teeth and hands, ignoring the spines on its hide. Despite an odor of rotten eggs, onions and spoiled meat, Uta thrust her hand deep into the custardy yellow pulp. She scooped fruit and stones into her mouth, and smacked her lips as she savored the treat. Once she stuck out her lower lip, full of food, and stared at it with comically crossed eyes, checking to see if all the pulp had been scraped off the seeds by her sturdy molars. Mawa stared too, hoping for her share.

Next the two visited a strangler fig. Long ago a bird had dropped a seed in the crotch of a tree. Drinking the moisture in the niche where it lay, the seed grew and sent down roots to the ground. The fig thrived on nourishment sucked up from the earth until it smothered the tree that supported it. Now the dead trunk was almost hidden by the rank growth of its ungrateful guest.

A great black male orang in the fig paid no attention to Uta's arrival. She also ignored him, since he was calmly eating, not aggressively calling. A troop of monkeys, two dark squirrels and flocks of pigeons came and went during the morning, tasting the figs.

Below, a family of wild pigs rooted among the fallen bits of fruit. Uta did not seem to like their tusked and bristly faces. She shook branches, unintentionally sending them a windfall of fruit. By sucking in her breath through pursed lips, she gave warning squeaks, but the pigs paid no attention.

All the visitors left the fig in the noontime heat. The forest seemed to rest as Uta and Mawa took their midday nap.

When they returned to the vine later, the black male was already there. A shy, sandy, little orang climbed up the fig root ladder. She was only three or four years old and weighed less than fifty pounds.

Female orangutans stay with their mothers longer than their brothers do. Perhaps, as they watch their mothers with new infants, they learn how to care for babies of their own. When a mature ape gives birth she is all alone, although her range may be close to her mother's.

The sandy stranger was unusually young to be foraging by herself. She still had the pale eyelids of babyhood. The "eye flash" made when such little orangutans blink is thought to be a signal to older apes, telling them the small ones are helpless and harmless.

The black male accepted her as he did other animals drawn to the fruitful vine. Clacking hornbills roosted, and a gibbon family grabbed figs as they swung through the branches. Then a sub-adult male orang began to climb the roots. The older one, no longer tolerant, watched the newcomer approach. A bubbling threat rose in his throat. His younger rival fled.

The little female followed Uta and Mawa for several days. Sometimes the two small apes played by themselves, although each knew the other was there. Sometimes Mawa pursued her new companion up and down and all around the tree crowns, and the orphan chased her in return. But when Mawa scooted back to her mother for a hug, her friend waited. She seemed a little afraid of Uta.

In the middle of one vigorous game of tag, Mawa's playmate gave a sudden squeal of terror. Jumping back from a snake coiled around a sunny stretch of branch, she slipped, fell and was lost in the leaves. Later the young ape climbed back awkwardly into the tree, with one crooked arm hanging limp. She did not stay with Mawa any longer, but moved away alone.

Despite the orangutans' caution as they travel through their lofty world, falls do happen. Bodies of the apes show large numbers of knitted bones. Although the lonely young lady's arm would heal, her carefree games of tag were probably finished.

Slaughtering
the Beast

T HE MILD MANNERED ORANGU-
tan of Dr. Abel, who tried to escape his per-
secutors, was very different from the usual picture of a
savage beast. Edgar Allan Poe used this ugly image in his
story "The Murders in the Rue Morgue." The villain of
the story cruelly killed two women. He was an orangutan.
Monsieur C. Auguste Dupin, the French equivalent of
Sherlock Holmes, solved the case, deducing that the
murders had been done by a creature "of an agility as-
tounding, a strength superhuman, a ferocity brutal, a
butchery without motive, a *grotesquerie* in horror abso-
lutely alien from humanity."

The most important clues were a tuft of tawny hair

The frightening, bloodthirsty orang from Poe's "Murders in the
Rue Morgue" brandishes an old-fashioned razor and a lock of hair
from one of his victims.

clutched by one of the victims and the finger marks on the throat of the other. No human hand fit the marks, but they matched perfectly the measurements of an orangutan's hand recorded earlier by the Baron de Cuvier.

Despite accounts of the orangutan's gentleness by Abel and others who had seen one, the bloodthirsty picture persisted. More was being learned from lifeless apes than from living ones at the time. And even an unimaginative person might find a resemblance between the body of a monstrous male orang and the threatening ogres of childhood fairy tales. The dead apes could not defend their reputations.

Although an understanding of the orangutan's personality and behavior could not be obtained from the many corpses imported into western countries, these specimens, and those of countless other animals and plants, did make possible the scientific achievements of the nineteenth century in sorting and classifying species. The confusions of the eighteenth century were clarified. The knowledge gained led to the next step in research; the twentieth century studies of living orangutans in zoos, laboratories and, most recently, in the rain forests.

The orangutan was a particular prize for the explorer-hunter in the last half of the nineteenth century simply because it was an ape. People began to show great curiosity about their nearest kin after the publication in 1859 of Charles Darwin's work on evolution, *On the Origin of Species*.

While Darwin was perfecting his theories, another Englishman, Alfred Russel Wallace, wrote a paper called *On the Tendency of Varieties to Depart Indefinitely from the Original Type.* Since he was then living in a thatched hut in Borneo, Wallace sent his paper to Darwin in England. It proposed that species changed through evolution.

Darwin was surprised that the same theory had been developed by someone else at the same time. But he was an honorable man. When he first presented his theories to a natural history society in 1858, he also read Wallace's paper to the group.

Meanwhile Wallace continued to study the animals and vegetation of the far eastern island—and to collect specimens. The efficiency of the rifle enabled him to slaughter orangutans hiding in the treetops with ease.

Wallace also adopted a very young orangutan. It was still toothless. While retrieving the corpse of an ape he had shot, he found a tiny infant face down in the mud, dropped by its dead mother. As he picked it up, the abandoned orphan wound its fingers into his full beard until Wallace thought that he would never be able to disentangle it.

The scientist took care of his baby with great tenderness. The ape had a box comfortably fitted out as a crib and had regular baths. Wallace even provided him with a foster mother, a bundle of buffalo skins to which he could cling. Unfortunately but naturally, he also tried to nurse. The baby choked on a mouthful of fur. "Mother" had to go. Instead, for a companion, Wallace obtained a young monkey named Toby. Toby used his larger friend as a pillow, sitting on his head or belly. The orang did not object as long as he had a warm object to hug.

In the frontispiece of
Wallace's book, *The
Malay Archipelago*, an
orangutan surrounded by
hunters fights for its life.

The childless Wallace had heard friends proudly prais-
ing their own offspring. He once wrote a long letter telling
about the charms and intelligence of his orangutan. After
four pages of this he ended, "You will see that my baby is
no common baby, and I can truthfully say, what so many
have said before with much less truth, 'There never was
such a baby as my baby.' "

The infant drank rice water and coconut milk. Wallace
spoonfed him biscuits mixed with sugar and eggs. But
there was no real milk available. The baby sickened and
died in three months.

Despite his interest in this one young ape, Wallace's
concern did not extend to all of the animals. He wrote,
"One of these we shot and killed . . . remained high up
in the fork of a tree; and, as young animals are of compara-

tively little interest, I did not have the tree cut down to get it."

A Dr. William Hornaday was also busy killing large numbers of orangutans. Hornaday was a taxidermist working for an establishment that sold specimens to schools and museums. On a single trip in 1897 he shot forty-three of the red apes. One successful day he managed to kill seven, from adults to a baby who made the mistake of peering over its nest at the strangers.

When the taxidermist was asked how he could stand dissecting such mounds of flesh, surrounded by a carpet of shaggy hides and watched by an audience of grinning skeletons, he explained that he "would not have exchanged the pleasures of that day . . . for a box at the opera the whole season through."

Later Dr. Hornaday became a dedicated conservationist. He was a founder of the National Zoo in Washington and the first president of the New York Zoological Society. When the Society started its zoo in the Bronx, there were more animals than buildings to house them, and no room for the first three orangutans. Mrs. Hornaday became their foster mother.

The River

their time in the forest canopy. Sometimes the mother
wrapped her arms and legs around the smooth trunk of a
tree and hitched herself down to the forest floor, with the
baby clinging to her back.

On one trip to earth, Uta seemed to have something in
mind. She hurried off in a determined direction, placing
her fists on the ground and then swinging her legs through
them. She gave up this crutching gait when she reached a
dense jungle of undergrowth. Thorny canes, bushes, palms
and eager saplings struggled for space in a spot of light.

The orangutan found a path through the tangle,
smoothed by the huge feet of elephants. It was lined with
dangling branches, broken when the browsing beasts tore
at the foliage. The trail led to a river where the elephants

57

went to drink and wallow. Muddy patches decorated trees where the gray giants had leaned to scratch their hides on their way back into the woods.

Mawa and Uta passed a clear circular area, the dancing ground of a male argus pheasant. Here he flaunts his long tail and iridescent wings to attract a mate. His dance ends with a rattle as he folds his wings, but he soon begins again. If disturbed, he streaks away down escape paths made through the underbrush. Predators, as well as female pheasants, are attracted by his flashy, noisy display.

Further along the trail, the orangutans faced another creature, a walking bundle of spines. As it ambled forward, the porcupine made a warning rattle. A cluster of hollow quills in its tail clacked and chattered, reminding other animals that it was too prickly to be fit for food.

The experienced Uta respected the message. She moved her curious daughter to the side of the path while the porcupine passed. As the two continued their trip, Uta went more slowly, walking on her fists and the sides of her curled feet.

A small stream blocked their way to the river. Uta, squatting by it, pursed her flexible lips into a funnel and sucked up the water. Then she ranged along the stream bank until she found a tree fallen over it. After the orangutans carefully crossed this natural bridge to the other side of the rivulet, they went back to rejoin the path.

Small trees and abundant bushes thrived in the sunlight at the river's edge. Uta was able to walk erect, holding onto low-growing branches for balance. Now and then, as she passed under a fruit-bearing bush, she plucked a bite to eat. Mawa, too short to reach the food, held her hand out to her mother. When Uta ignored her appeal, the baby collapsed on the ground into a round red bundle. She beat the earth with her fists. She screamed. But her mother kept moving until Mawa, terrified of being left behind, forgot her tantrum and raced down the path. Casually, as if the scene had not occurred, Uta passed a piece of fruit to her daughter, without stopping or missing a step. She was still searching for something.

When the orangutan reached a patch of hard red ground between chalky rocks, she had found her goal. She scooped up some of the mineral-rich earth into her mouth.

While her mother satisfied an instinctive need for calcium, sodium and potassium, Mawa stared at the broad brown river. Sleek heads of playful otters appeared and disappeared in the sluggish swirls of the current. On the shore, a six-foot monitor lizard basked on a warm boulder. An electric-blue kingfisher rocketed out of the woods to patrol the waters. A rare rhinoceros wallowed in the mud near the far shore.

Closer, a damp patch of sand brought Rajah butterflies to drink the seeping moisture. Their broad wings cloaked the ground in black velvet sparked by yellow streaks. Because they lived low in the still depths of the forest, they could have larger wings than the butterflies that fought the winds as they flew.

Thirst slaked and her craving for minerals satisfied, Uta turned away from the river. Mawa followed her into the shadowy woods. Soon they would rejoin the birds and squirrels and smaller butterflies in the breezy treetops.

In the Zoo

AS THE NINETEENTH CENTURY BE-
came the twentieth, attention turned to liv-
ing orangutans instead of dead ones. People flocked to zoos
to watch their fellow primates behind bars.

Capturing orangutans rather than killing them did not
help the apes themselves. Babies, easy to handle and trans-
port, were in the greatest demand. But catching a baby
meant killing its mother.

After a poacher disentangled an infant from its mother's
fur, he took it back to his hut until he could find a dealer
to buy it. In primitive villages, captured orangs were often
chained below the stilted houses. They lived in mud and
ate rice diluted with water. If dampness or illness did not
kill them, the poor diet did.

Not all the babies died or the trade would have been too unprofitable to continue. It is estimated that about half of the captives did reach new homes abroad. For every orang that arrived safely, though, at least three were lost— another baby and the two mothers. Some scientists think that the proportion is even greater—four or five dead for each young one that arrived to amuse spectators.

The little apes were not amusing for long. Only one in five lived to be three, and an orang that young is still a child without permanent teeth. At the London Zoo the average life span of their twenty orangutans was only five-and-a-half months.

At first no one knew how to care for the infants or what to feed them. Bare cement cages offered none of the comforts of the leafy rain forest and few opportunities to exercise. Even the zoo goers who came to see the orangutans were sometimes responsible for their deaths. One youngster who wasted away in San Diego was found to have its stomach stuffed with gum, even the wrappers, during the autopsy.

The great apes share many of our diseases. They are particularly susceptible to respiratory infections. In the winter of 1913–1914 sick visitors started an epidemic of tuberculosis which swept through the Bronx Zoo's collection of nine orangutans and chimpanzees, killing them all.

Today most great apes are displayed behind thick glass rather than bars, to protect the valuable animals from both germs and mistaken gifts of harmful foods. But illness can still race through a zoo like lightning. In 1965 a famous collection of orangutans in Europe was almost wiped out

Young Andy sucks his sore toe while waiting for the doctor at the Bronx Zoo. Increased knowledge about orangutans means that they can receive excellent medical care in zoos today.

by smallpox, not human but monkey pox.

Illness is not the only problem of captive orangs. They become bored. Pacing tigers, yawning lions and many other creatures show signs of boredom in zoos, but it is the most intelligent of all, the apes, who most need challenges to their minds and bodies. "Stereotyped behavior" is the name scientists use for senseless and repeated acts forced on captive animals by their inactivity. Gorillas tear out their hair, strand by strand, for years until their forearms are completely bare. A chimpanzee in the Staten Island Zoo retires to a corner of the cage and bangs its head on the floor there with clocklike regularity.

Some zoos have put on afternoon "tea parties" to keep their young primates busy and to entertain the public. Perhaps the people are more amused than the apes. They love to watch animals behave as humans, and chimpanzees, at least, love to be watched. These extroverted hams revel in applause—and in aping their audiences.

But the shy and solitary orangutan is another animal. Long ago the Bronx Zoo had a show with orangs among the actors. They ate sliced bananas neatly with forks, poured their milk, used toothpicks, lit cigarettes, smoked and spat. They rode tricycles and donned and doffed items of their masters' clothing.

Three orangs went through their tricks docilely, if not with enthusiasm. The fourth, an individualist named Dohong, apparently considered smoking and spitting and wearing clothes no concern of a proper orangutan. The zookeepers found that he was more of a mechanical genius than an actor.

Unenthusiastic ape actors pose for their portraits. In the foreground a worried little orangutan nibbles his finger and two youngsters, chimp and orang, hug each other for reassurance.

Dohong was fascinated by the equipment in his cage. He investigated all the ropes and exercise bars repeatedly. Sometimes he put them to imaginative use. A metal piece of his trapeze proved handy in prying apart the bars of his cage.

Dohong's mechanical aptitude is typical of orangs. A young one named Bob, newly arrived at the San Diego Zoo, promptly untwisted the wire netting of his cage. He had already shoved his blankets and toys through the hole when he was discovered. He evidently had not planned on returning. But when he was caught, the affectionate escape artist just held up his arms for a hug.

When put into a sturdier cage, Bob got out as easily and went to play with some neighboring penguins. His next home was a heavy cage, which had successfully held lions and grizzly bears. But not Bob. He worked one of the bars loose and celebrated with a night in the room where food was stored, helping himself to all the grapes, apples and bananas he wanted.

Bob was skillful and clever, but young. When this dexterity is combined with the awesome strength of an adult orang, the results can be disastrous.

The Bronx Zoo had a three-hundred-pound male, Briggs. In the early 1970s, his cement and steel cage was transformed into something closer to a natural jungle habitat. There were artificial trunks and branches for climbing and heavy metal cables in the place of vines.

Briggs considered his new environment a challenge rather than a happy forest home. He wrested loose the branches bolted to the walls and twisted the cables as if

Briggs exploring— before destroying —his jungle habitat.

they really were slender vines. When a grape rolled through the floor, he ripped up the metal grillwork trying to retrieve it.

An air conditioning vent was set in a stout steel frame flush with the ceiling so that the ingenious ape could not get a grip on it. That was the plan. Briggs thought otherwise. He patiently chipped at the cement until he could hook his fingers around the frame. Down came the vent, and Briggs was busily taking it to pieces when his mischief was discovered. So the orangutan returned to a cement cell while humans tried again to build an ape-proof jungle.

Such clever and curious animals obviously need as much equipment as possible—jungle gyms, swinging ropes and a variety of toys. But their curiosity also makes this difficult. They will investigate everything, which means that they will dismantle, bend, break and destroy everything. The best zoos seem to be able to do is provide some climbing apparatus of sturdy chains and strong, sleek steel. Because such materials are unchangeable, though, they are of little lasting interest to orangutans.

The Rains

IN NOVEMBER, MONSOONS FROM THE northwest swept over the forest. The rainy season had begun.

The woods darkened by midafternoon as black-bellied clouds sailed across the sky. Wind-whipped branches groaned and creaked, but other sounds stopped. Even the birds and ceaselessly singing insects seemed to be waiting.

As the first drops spat on the leaves, Uta retreated to the day nest she had made for her nap. Nearby Mawa was experimenting with twigs and soft switches, folding them together into a practice nest. At the rattle of rain, she dropped down to hang from a branch beneath her ragged structure. When the full flood of the storm shredded her umbrella, the soaking baby hurried to her mother's side.

66

Uta pulled branches over the nest and, in this makeshift hut, the two spent the night as the storm blew and blustered. Gradually the lightning dimmed and the thunder grew dull and distant. Uta and Mawa slept.

Mist trailed through the trees in the morning. Although the rain was over, a gentle patter continued as drops slipped through the many-layered canopy. Uta tore handfuls of wet leaves from their roof to quench her thirst.

As the light grew stronger the two apes climbed up to sunbathed branches higher in the tree. There they basked in the warmth while their wet fur steamed.

After they were dry, the orangutans set out to satisfy their hunger. They worked their way down to the damp earth. Uta rolled a rotting log over and poked at the sodden wood with a long finger, searching for grubs.

Water filled a hole made when a falling tree ripped its roots from the ground. Mawa splashed her hands in the shallow stuff and stirred it into a muddy custard. Then she noticed that Uta's explorations had succeeded. She was pulling grubs from their spongy refuge. A couple of somersaults brought Mawa to her mother's side, and breakfast.

The torrential rains went on and on, pouring almost six feet of water into the forest during November, December and January. The supply of fruit dwindled. In February, it made up less than a quarter of Uta's meals. She spent increasing time tearing the tough cover from branches and scraping the tender inner bark off with her broad buck teeth. After sucking all the juices from the pulp, she spat out cuds of shredded wood.

Mawa and Uta's routine of feeding, travel and rest began

to be interrupted less often by rain. February brought only half as much as stormy, soggy January, and in March only nine inches fell. But the orangutans were still dependent on leaves and lianas for most of their food.

Some of the vines Uta chewed drooled gummy sap that hung in threads from her chin. During rest times she cleaned herself, removing the sticky beard, scratching her chest or poking a finger through the long hair on her arms. Chimpanzees spend many hours grooming each other for reasons more social than sanitary. The isolated adult orang-utans have seldom been seen to do this. Uta did inspect Mawa's fur at first, but as the baby grew she became less thorough in caring for her.

Mawa's birthday was in March. During the two years of her life, she had first watched what her mother ate. Soon after her birth she had begun tasting samples dropped by Uta. Then she had followed the older ape's example in choosing food. Now she knew what was best for orangutans among all the offerings of the forest. She was weaned from her dependence on milk, but Uta would still allow her to suckle at times until the arrival of another baby.

The mother was now making it harder for her daughter to hitch a ride. When Uta decided to move from one feeding spot, she strode off to the next, leaving the whimpering youngster to scamper after her. Mawa was able to travel under her own power, but not always willing.

Slowly, like all higher primates, the little orang was growing up.

Dim Hope Without a Tree—a Flea

ENERGETIC YOUNG ORANGUTANS can amuse themselves in almost any environment. At the Philadelphia Zoo, four of them live in two tiled cages, each with a metal shelf, exercise bar and water basin. The adolescent apes, five and six years old, turn these sterile cubes into circus rings.

Sara and Yakut chase and shove each other. They wrestle, bite—and then settle down for a rest, holding hands. After chewing leaves from fresh branches provided daily, Bagong and Mania pass the food from mouth to mouth.

Each also plays alone in true orangutan fashion, climbing, swinging and somersaulting. Sara enjoys curling up on her back and spinning around and around in a carrot-

Sara and Yakut press their heads against the glass of their cage while posing for photographers. The smeary, finger-painted glass may show the apes' inborn artistry—or just their playfulness.

colored blur. Another will sit in a corner, gathering branches and straw as if making a nest—until its companion steals the building material to pile on its head.

Unlike the unenthusiastic actors at tea parties, these antic orangs delight in showing off tricks of their own invention. A favorite is hurling handfuls of water at their audience. Although protected by glass, the onlookers always flinch. Maybe the apes are teasing their superior relatives.

The orangutans notice anyone who watches them for a long time, especially someone with a camera. They cluster close to the glass in front of the photographer and jostle for the best position. If one appears to be stealing the scene, another will make outlandish faces, try a handstand or even spit a cud of half-chewed food on the glass—and then peer coyly around the mess to see what effect it is having.

Meanwhile the apes in the adjoining cage knock briskly on the glass. It is their turn for the spotlight.

Adult orangs are naturally less active and curious than their babies. It takes a greater incentive to keep them exercised and alert. The ideal zoo environment would be one where they could climb, search for food and build nests as they do in the wild. Being trapped in cages is more harmful for these arboreal apes than for the partly terrestrial chimps and gorillas.

Without natural activity, male orangutans can lapse into tragic states. They huddle on shelves in the corners of their cages, faces turned to the walls. All visitors can see is a massive pile of ropey red hair. And only food arouses them from this stupor.

Sara's handstand proves an excellent way to attract attention. Visitors always laugh at her acrobatics.

The lack of exercise tends to make the grown males tremendously obese. They develop fatty crests on their heads, exaggerated pouches and bulging bellies. An idle zoo male can become twice as heavy as even the barrel-chested forest ones. Such grotesque giants appeal to some zoo goers, perhaps ones who also visit freak shows, but the poor creatures are lazy and listless. Some even have difficulty hoisting their huge bodies to stand or walk.

This monstrous burden of fat interferes with mating. The best argument for keeping orangutans in zoos is for breeding. They are endangered animals. It is essential that they mate successfully and that their offspring live and grow and breed themselves. So obesity hurts the species as well as individuals.

Although orangutans have been in zoos since the Princes of Orange received them as gifts, it was not until 1928 that the first babies were born in captivity, two in Germany and one in Philadelphia. All three died. Their mothers' milk was inadequate, probably because of an improper diet during the months before they gave birth. For years so little was known about the proper care of the apes that few survived long enough to become parents. And orangutans can be choosey about their mates.

At the Philadelphia Zoo, young Bung and Goolah were a contented pair. Then, after Goolah gave birth, Bung was removed from her cage to protect the baby. He set up housekeeping with Christine instead, and fathered three children. Since Christine was an indifferent mother and would not care for her babies, they were raised by human volunteers. Bung remained with her.

Big Bung in action, striding along his shelf. His broad buck teeth are well adapted to scraping fruit from their rinds. Orangutans also have strong wide molars to rasp the pulp from fruit pits.

After Goolah's maternal duties were over, the zoo staff reintroduced Bung into her cage, hoping that another infant would result. The huge adult male, however, did not resemble the handsome mate she had known several years before. Afraid, Goolah would have nothing to do with him. Bung returned to Christine while a younger male was borrowed from another zoo for Goolah.

Although Bung is an impressive figure as a full adult, he is not the obese caricature that some males become. He still moves from shelf to floor with ease and swings on the bar. The Philadelphia orangs are kept in trim with a special diet devised at the zoo many years ago and now used around the world. The main course is zoo cake, a moist loaf of cereals, meat, vitamins and minerals. Carrots, kale, cabbage and other leafy vegetables provide the salad, while dessert is fruit—apples, oranges, raisins, watermelon.

The meals for the apes are carefully rationed according to body size and activity. Growing young orangutans get a

Christine enjoying her zoo cake, a nourishing and balanced food perhaps people should try.

half ounce of food a day for each pound they weigh. The quieter adults receive from a quarter to a tenth of an ounce. With this controlled and balanced diet, premature deaths from malnutrition or obesity no longer occur. The orangs live until their hearts, kidneys or other vital organs wear out with age.

Two of the Philadelphia orangutans have broken all records for longevity. Guarina died in 1976 at fifty-six and her mate, Gua, is still alive at the same age.

This venerable pair also broke breeding records. Guarina, who had already had one baby in 1929 before coming to Philadelphia, produced eight infants fathered by Gua, including Bung's companion, Christine.

In 1964 the total number of orangutans born in zoos was only about five a year, but more of the apes are following the example of Christine and Guarina today. Forty zoos now have breeding pairs. Perhaps the captive orangs are no longer endangered, but, if the wild ones should disappear, will we really have saved the orangutan? Is the zoo inhabitant the same creature as the shy nomad of the rain forest?

One man who knows the orangs well does not think so. Tom Harrisson lived in Borneo, where he and his wife, Barbara, played parents to orphaned little apes. Harrisson mourned the life of an orangutan behind bars, "To an Orang . . . there is dim hope where there is no tree, no butterfly, no flea! Orangs love and live for trees, leaves, mucking about, investigating, worrying, irregular rhythms, natural jokes."

The Mate

THE CONSTANT TEMPERATURES OF the rain forest meant that there was no summer or winter, no spring or fall. The time when each tree burst into bloom depended on local conditions around it, not a predictable year-round cycle of weather. A tree on a river bank might bud after floods brought by the monsoons. Another, deeper in the woods, flowers in response to several dry weeks.

Wet times and dry ones alternated in the forest and another year went by. Mawa, at three, was increasingly independent during the day. At night she still shared her mother's nest.

The young orang did not realize that, as she grew up, Uta would mate again. Male orangutans, however, understood that this female, with a daughter able to care for herself, might be interested in their attentions.

One May day, as Uta and Mawa moved and munched through a forest still sparkling after a brief shower, a male with flaming red hair appeared, sub-adult and still agile. He swung through the trees swiftly in rhythmic arcs with the grace, if not the figure, of a dancer. After settling down not far from Uta, he managed to find food closer and closer to her during the afternoon. At night he built his nest near hers.

Uta was not interested in the sub-adult. In the morning she woke early and started walking briskly along a broad branch while her neighbor of the night was still asleep. As the limb tapered, Uta slid under it and proceeded hand over hand. The bough dipped with her weight and she easily reached down to another branch, pulling it in with her foot. On and on she went, her hungry daughter close behind. When her mother finally stopped to eat, Mawa copied her promptly.

Among the males Mawa had seen, the most familiar was a big black one who foraged near them now and then. He had not visited Uta's range for some time. Perhaps he had moved to more fertile feeding grounds. The adaptable orangutans can alter their ranges in response to changing conditions. Or perhaps the black male had died. He was close to forty.

Now an unfamiliar male was crossing the ground toward the little family. The dense hair falling from his head and shoulders, which never stopped growing, made a chocolate-colored cape. Above it loomed his swollen face. The growth of cheek flanges, thick parentheses of fatty tissue, had broadened his face until his features became those of a wizened little man in a large moon. Underlining this frightening countenance, a pouch hung in a wrinkled hammock across his chest.

The newcomer hunched across the forest floor. The great weight of the grown males forces them to do much of their travelling on the ground, and this chocolate fellow was monstrous.

When he reached the base of Uta's tree, he pulled himself up to his full four feet and wrapped his long arms around the trunk. Their eight-foot span circled it firmly. He thrust with his short bowed legs and moved his arms a little further up the tree. Heels against the bark, he pushed again, inching his way up the trunk until he reached a crotch made by the first strong branch. There he sat securely, breaking boughs and pulling foliage toward himself to eat.

Mawa expected her mother to flee this grim sight, as she had males before, but Uta continued to feed while slowly edging downward nearer the chocolate orang. Night found them both in the tree, where Uta built a lower nest than usual.

In the early light of the next day, Mawa was terrified to see a brown-framed face rise over the side of the nest. As the male poked Uta experimentally, the baby screamed and beat him on the chest. Uta screamed too, just once. Encouraged, her suitor started to climb into the nest despite the blows from Mawa's tiny fists. Neither adult noticed her tantrum.

The unwanted young one left the crowded nest, but she did not go far. She sipped dew from moss and nibbled on fern fronds, ignoring the grunts, squeals and childish behavior of her elders. During the next few days, Mawa learned not to fear the male's trumpeting calls, announcing his possession of a mate. Although still jealous, she became used to her mother's silly behavior and attentive friend.

Then the chocolate orangutan left as abruptly as he had arrived. The remaining two took up their quiet routine again with only each other for company.

In the Laboratory

IN 1964 ONLY 278 ORANGUTANS
lived in the zoos of the world. Ten years later
the number had grown to 625. And these are not all of
the captive orangs, for others are used in scientific research.
The closeness of apes to people make the animals ideal
subjects for studies of our illnesses, our addictions and our
physical and psychological needs.

The superior brain of human beings is the greatest
difference between them and their primate relatives. But
which of the great apes is the brightest? Most people probably think of the popular, extroverted chimpanzee as the
Einstein of the animal world, but no one really knows.

The forthright personality of the chimp may have as

An orangutan smoking. Great apes exposed to human habits can form similar addictions.

much to do with its success in solving problems and doing tricks as its intelligence. It attacks a puzzle eagerly and either solves it—or vents its frustration in a furious tantrum. The careful orangutan approaches anything new in its life with a very different attitude.

One time a scientist showed a picture of an alligator to all three of the great apes. The bold chimps hurried to get a close look at the strange creature. They even poked fingers through the wire of their cage to touch it.

The gorillas quietly watched what was happening from a distance of eight to ten feet.

The frightened orangutans backed even further away or scooted into their enclosed inner cages. They did not return until the threatening beast was gone.

The red apes also become interested in the wrong part of tests from the scientists' point of view. They explore the equipment instead of solving the problems. Four orangs learned several simple ways to obtain food—pulling it in with a rake or stick or string, moving some obstacle to reach it and opening a box to find the reward. The five chimpanzees in the experiment succeeded in these tasks and also in a sixth, unbolting a box. But the orangutans were more

In a test at the Yerkes Research Center, Gahgah concentrates on getting some candy by pushing it out of a tube with a stick.

interested in the operation of the bolt than the food inside the box. They just played with the hardware.

It has been suggested that the orangutan's mechanical aptitude stems from inborn abilities needed in its wild life. The apes have to understand spatial relationships and be able to judge alternate routes through the trees to reach out-of-the-way clusters of fruit. They are also accustomed to handling sticks, which they break off and drop when they are upset.

One orang, unable to get to a tree, pulled it close with a hooked branch—the nearest approach to tool-using observed in the wild. Captive orangutans certainly use tools without training, particularly anything that could act as a lever to spread the bars of their cages.

In addition to playing mechanic instead of student, orangutans have other ways of confusing the results of experiments. A scientist tried to train some of the apes to place red, yellow and blue blocks on spots of matching colors. They did well, but not because they knew red, yellow and blue. Their teacher soon realized that his pupils were slyly watching him for clues as to what they should do. The same orangs were able to choose the right key out of a dozen for each door in the house where they lived. Opening doors was a more rewarding activity than playing with blocks.

One ability of both chimps and orangs has surprised the people who studied them. Although scientists thought the problem would be too much for the apes, psychologists tested them in "cross-modal" transfer. Humans recognize things through more than one sense. A blindfolded person can tell an orange through touch, taste, or smell, in place of sight. The identification of something through first one sense and then another is a cross-modal transfer.

To test the chimpanzees and orangutans, scientists used pairs of objects with different shapes—for example, square boxes, round balls and triangular blocks. One of each pair was hidden in a bag. Then the apes were shown one of the remaining objects—perhaps the ball. They could pick out the matching ball from the bag by feeling its roundness. To the observers' further surprise, some selected the ball by touch even if they had only seen a one-dimensional picture of it.

While a dog ignores a photograph of the juiciest steak unless it has a meaty smell, pictures are as real to apes as they are to us. There were those orangutans who fled from the painted alligator. Another one, an orphan raised by

Although orangutans recognize pictures, their own creations tend to be abstract. Alexander seems dismayed by his latest work.

humans, kissed photographs of people and tried to chew the flowers on his foster mother's skirt.

Orangutans interpret pictures as we do and are capable of cross-modal transfers. How intelligent are they? One infant scored 200 on an intelligence test meant for human babies. Tests for such little ones, though, consist of handling blocks and other physical tasks instead of the more complicated language problems of IQ tests for older children. The orang's amazing score probably resulted from the better coordination of young apes. They develop physical skills much earlier than human babies.

In 1916 Dr. Robert M. Yerkes ran many experiments with an orangutan in his laboratory. If the ape, Julius, walked through the one correct box out of nine, he found a reward of fruit on its other side. The often tired and discouraged orang never did solve the problem with any regularity. Monkeys, and even pigs, did better than Julius. But Yerkes felt that the lower animals learned by trial-and-error, while Julius was attempting, even if unsuccessfully, to use his reasoning powers to discover the prize.

This independent ape also would not use the stick provided by the scientist to knock down a bunch of bananas hanging at the top of his cage. But he still got his fruit. Inventive Julius turned the stick into a vaulting pole, which lifted him within reach of the treat.

At the Yerkes laboratory today, Dr. Duane M. Rumbaugh has been working with all three great apes to find out how they learn and how much. One series of tests also involved monkeys and the lesser apes, gibbons. The animals were taught to do one thing to earn a reward, such as selecting a square from a choice of square and circle.

When they picked the proper shape regularly, the test was reversed. The animals had to choose the circle to be rewarded. All the great apes understood the changed conditions more easily than the other primates. Interestingly, the gorillas and orangutans did better than the chimpanzees.

For a second experiment, Dr. Rambaugh used three pairs of apes. One orangutan and one chimpanzee made each pair.

The first group was taught a number of tasks—taking a candy out of a container, carrying an object from one place to another, hunting for something hidden, putting different-sized containers inside each other in the right order and inserting a piece of plastic into a hole of the same shape cut out of a wooden board. The apes had three of these puzzles to solve, each with a different figure—a rectangle, a triangle and a circle. They were trained with many objects in varied colors, sizes and materials.

The second group learned the same tasks, but the two apes had just one bowl for the candy, one thing to carry or find, one set of cannisters and a single, rectangular puzzle.

The third pair were the control group. They spent just as much time with the materials as the first two, but no one showed them what to do with the things.

Rumbaugh wanted to find out if the apes accustomed to a large variety of objects would be the best at solving problems with new materials and handling unfamiliar items with imagination.

After the training period, the animals were given new objects and their skills in manipulating them were compared and recorded. Expectedly, the group I apes nested barrel halves, boxes and sets of cups more often than group II, and both those pairs did better than group III.

All of the apes had trouble with a new puzzle, a square. But the group I orangutan starred with a second, harder puzzle, needing both a circle and a jagged piece to fill the hole. She put it together in less than four minutes.

This same three-year-old female, Roberta, proved the most active and ingenious of the apes in the last test for "responsiveness." Each animal had a turn alone in an outside play yard with a stick, a paper bag, a cannister, a cup, a rope and two blocks. An observer noted how many times each ape "responded" to the objects.

One of the control group did not touch anything. Even

The two-piece puzzle which was solved only by the orang, Roberta.

the group I chimp only handled the objects six times. But Roberta earned the description, "particularly creative," as she put the lid on the cannister and took it off, held the cannister on her head, used it as a stool and packed and unpacked it repeatedly with not just the blocks but grass, pebbles and bits of paper torn from the bag. She acted with the various materials a total of fifty-two times.

Roberta was an especially bright individual. The personality and intelligence of each ape might have more effect on its abilities than whether it is a chimp, orang or gorilla.

Among the apes, as among us, there are geniuses and there are idiots. One poor little chimp, Jama, was born a Mongoloid. Until her condition was noticed when she was nine months old, no one had suspected that apes shared this human problem, which leads to mental retardation and physical defects. Jama developed at about half the rate of normal infant chimpanzees until her malformed heart failed and her short, distorted life was over.

Which primate does rank after humans in intelligence —the eager, active chimpanzee, the persistent and patient gorilla or the wary, introspective orangutan? Perhaps the brightest individuals of all three will have to share the title.

The Men

THE TWO ORANGUTANS WERE FEAST-
ing. Inspired to unusually acrobatic efforts, Uta managed
to reach a bees' nest hanging high in a towering mengaris
tree. There she celebrated, eating the syrup-coated wax
and soft grubs as well as the honey. Mawa was discovering
this concentrated sweetness and pleasure for the first time.

Angry bees swarmed from the remains of their pen-
dulous nest. Thickly furred Uta closed her eyes, and then
paid little attention. Now and then she waved an arm at
the buzzing cloud, but the sweet treat mattered more than
the noisy protesters.

The great heights where the bees nested protected their
honey to some extent. But this tree was scored with grooves

made by the sharp claws of sun bears as they climbed the branchless trunk to the prize above.

The members of local tribes also coveted the honey. Without the orangutans' agility or the bears' claws, it took even greater efforts for them to get it. At the foot of the mengaris, poles and pegs were already piled in preparation for a raid on the nests. They would be tied together into a shaky ladder inching slowly up the tree.

A man walked toward this cache with a hefty rope over one shoulder. Made of the braided stems of a climbing palm, it was sturdy enough to hold the heavy buckets of honey as they were lowered to the ground.

After darkness came to cloak the approach to the nest, the man planned to return with friends. They would bring the last supplies—buckets, lianas to tie the poles, and torches to drive the bees away from their combs. Then, after all the long preparations, the raiders would build their ladder and claim the loot.

The bees disturbed by Uta were swooping about in anger. They discovered the new interloper and attacked instinctively, furiously. Thinking about his plan, the man had not noticed the swarms until the first sharp sting. He dropped the rope and fled.

Another day Mawa found another new food. As she played by herself, the little ape saw a nesting bird cowering nearby. It sat utterly still as if it hoped to hide from the inquisitive youngster. When Mawa stuck out one exploring finger, the bird's courage collapsed. With a squawk it flapped off the nest and fled into the foliage. The orang stared with interest at the pale round eggs left unguarded.

The bird's cry brought Uta over to her child. She recognized the eggs as edible, and they were gone before Mawa had a chance to taste them. But the young one had learned and would be sure to share in the contents of the next nest. Meanwhile the orang amused herself plucking at this one, dropping twigs and grass to float in the breeze.

As Uta and Mawa returned to their more usual harvesting of fruit, they were joined by dark-faced, red-haired Oora, Uta's first offspring, now an adult. Mawa had seen her sister several times before. Where Oora's range overlapped her mother's, she followed the same paths and visited the same trees she had known in her infancy. When the two females met, they sometimes travelled together for a day or two.

Now Oora was no longer alone. A tiny face peered out from under her arm. Entranced, Mawa crept close to investigate, but Oora grunted sternly and shifted the baby to her other side. Perhaps she was worried about her infant, but the new mother did not stay long before moving off on her own.

A man watched this scene through his binoculars and tried to interpret it. Suddenly, Uta noticed the strange human with great black bug eyes jutting from his face. She rose and shook the branches around her. Tearing one off, she swung it in a circle and then let it fall heavily to the ground. The man did not move. Uta dropped more branches, while expressing her irritation with grumbles, gulps and grunts. She slowly ran out of complaints as she watched what he was doing.

The bug eyes had fallen from his face. The man was

calmly chewing a leaf. Then he dropped to his knees and began to gather long grass and loose twigs around himself. Could this odd animal be building a nest?

He did not seem dangerous, and the tree was too fruitful to leave. Uta moved discreetly deeper into the branches, until the thick trunk and dense greenery shielded her from the man, maybe peaceful but certainly puzzling. Although she was safe this time, perhaps even wary Uta was not timid enough.

In the Field

SINCE THE MID-60S, BINOCULAR-bearing ethologists, scientists who study animals in the field instead of in the laboratory or dissection room, have pursued orangutans.

Before that time very little was known about the natural life of the apes. Although many questions remain, much has been learned by the hardy men and women who slog through swamps and forests to study their fellow primates.

Dr. John MacKinnon first introduced orangutans to many people with his book, *In Search of the Red Ape*. It tells about his experiences in the field and the orangutans he watched for over fifteen hundred hours in Borneo and Sumatra.

He went by boat down the Segama river deep into the forests of an area called Sabah in northern Borneo. Local tribesmen accompanied him to pilot the boats, bring in supplies, cook the food and vary it by hunting and fishing. One meal MacKinnon will not forget was monkey stew. He expected a welcome relief from canned goods until he saw the animal's face grinning up at him from the gravy.

MacKinnon lived on a wooden platform without walls, but with a thatched roof to ward off the rains. When following an ape, however, he slept out in the jungle so that he would be close when the animal rose from its nest in the morning. By leaving caches of food and plastic sheets for shelter in the woods, he was able to travel as freely as the unburdened orangs.

There were dangers in the wilderness: sharp-toothed crocodiles, irritable boars and the rare cattle, banteng, with males as big as buffalo and bad-tempered as bulls. Elepants crashing through the dark could trample a person bedded down for the night. MacKinnon learned to make his sleeping quarters at the bases of tall trees whose trunks broadened into sturdy, supporting buttresses. Between these walls of wood, the scientist was safe.

As MacKinnon travelled through the forest, swamps sucked at his legs and barbed vines ripped his skin. Mosquitoes bit, wasps stung and leeches were everywhere, waiting in the damp undergrowth to gorge on the blood of passersby. There were cobras and vipers, thirty species of poisonous snakes in all. Luckily for the researcher on the ground, these reptiles were mostly arboreal.

MacKinnon makes himself at home in his rain forest camp.

Once MacKinnon was attacked by an irate sun bear who was defending her cub. Even occasional orangutans became angered at his persistence and climbed down to chase him away.

Despite danger, heat, humidity and fevers and wounds for which MacKinnon himself was the only doctor, the scientist continued his study of the apes. Other dedicated ethologists have also contributed valuable information.

Through their work we have learned much about the nesting and feeding habits of orangs, their vocalizations, gestures and expressions—all things that make up the story of Mawa. But many questions about the red apes, particularly about their social behavior, remain.

If an ethologist in Africa sights a chimpanzee or gorilla,

the chances are that other animals are nearby. Since these social apes live together, interactions between different ones can be observed almost continuously.

But in Asia, the orangutans' solitary lives provide limited opportunities to study their social relations. Sometimes numbers of the apes gather together in fruiting trees, but these are not really social occasions. The animals are interested in the ample amount of food available, not in each other. More truly social groups may consist of two or three immature orangs travelling together, a male and a female in a consortship or a pair of females with young, perhaps a mother and her grown daughter.

Even after an orangutan mother has borne a new infant, her previous child, if a female, may stay nearby for several years. Then, the daughter will spend gradually increasing amounts of time on her own, first with adolescent friends and later, alone. When she is ready to mate, she will have established her own range, although part of it will overlap her mother's.

The young males leave their mothers earlier and move further away than their sisters. Their travels ensure that they will be in another part of the forest when old enough to father babies. This prevents the inbreeding that would occur if the males also settled next to their mothers. There is some evidence that these wandering adolescents try to establish their importance, or dominance, among others of their own age.

At about ten, the male enters sub-adulthood. He is sexually mature, but does not yet have the completely

The strongest and longest lasting social bond among orangutans
is between mother and child.

developed flanges, pouch, and sometimes beard, of the adult male. His attempts to show dominance over other orangs become directed at adult females as well as at his peers. A sub-adult will mate, sometimes violently, with the females he meets in his travels. Some of the young males have been seen with the same females in stable consortships for long periods of time. But even these good companions seem unwilling to mate with their youthful escorts, and seek out fully adult males when they are ready to breed. The patriarchs of the forest apparently pass on their strengths to the next generations, while the younger apes' sexual activity relates more to dominance than reproduction.

It is possible that the males' long calls attract females when they are receptive and fertile. The calls are also believed to help in spacing these giants throughout the forest. Since they have overlapping ranges, it is important that each male know where others are, so that he can keep his distance. It would be dangerous to depend on sight rather than sound to locate potential rivals. When two adult males meet, a very real and vicious fight can take place, resulting in the scars often seen on many wild males, and possibly the deaths of a few. The large size of the males, perhaps once important in protecting prehistoric families, is now important in the competition between these giant animals.

This description of neighborly mothers and daughters, adolescent fellow travellers, sub-adults seeking dominance and aggressive adults suggests that orangutans lead a busy social life. But they spend much more time alone than in groups of any kind. Why are they so unlike the gregarious chimpanzees and gorillas?

All three of the great apes are large and need correspondingly large amounts of food. The biggest of all, the gorillas, have broad ranges within which they can find ample supplies of the wide variety of herbs, leaves, tree pulp, vines and other vegetables they eat.

Chimpanzees prefer the harder-to-find fruits. But there is no great size difference between male and female chimps. They both can get fair shares of what fruit is to be found. They also have other sources of nourishment. Chimpanzees are the only apes who have been seen to eat red meat, and even hunt and kill small animals, such as baby wild pigs and monkeys.

Orangutans do eat bark, leaves and other things when they must, but those foods are not sufficiently nourishing. Although they can store energy in their fat to help them through lean times, orangs need fruit. They travel slowly, and a troop of animals the size of orangutans, moving leisurely, would soon gobble up all the fruits of areas it passed through, with big males getting the greater portions. Single apes, or small families, can forage without devestating the forests. The crops can feed all the other creatures dependent on them, and still regenerate, year after year.

Since humans are the only predators threatening orangutans in Borneo, a female does not need masculine protection from other animals. It is better for her to live alone and not have to share the food in her range with a male too often.

Ranges of female orangutans average two-and-a-third

A wild male orang objects to MacKinnon disturbing his life as a hermit.

square miles in size. An adult male has a larger range that overlaps the home grounds of several females. As he moves from one to another seeking food, he is able to check on the reproductive states of the females he meets regularly during his rounds. After giving birth, a female will remain infertile for at least three years, and perhaps as long as five, while raising her infant. At this time she is apt to flee from grown males, as if in fear, and fight the attentions of sub-adults.

When her offspring is able to build nests and to travel and feed without help, the mother becomes fertile again and more interested in the adult males. She may well be attracted by not only their big size, long hair and dramatic posturings but also by their strange facial features, heavy pouches and broad cheeks. It does appear as if orangs ready to start the unending cycle of child bearing and caring again actually seek out these impressive creatures as partners. Once an adolescent female, ignored by the mate of her choice, was seen grooming him, a rare event in the life of an orang.

This seems to be the pattern of orangutan life emerging from research in the field by various ethologists, in studies taking many months and, sometimes, years. But observations of the red apes have still not accumulated the vast amount of information available on the other great apes.

Scientists have spent more time studying these African animals. Outstanding among them are Dian Fossey, who has watched mountain gorillas for ten years among the volcanoes of central Africa, and Jane Goodall. For fifteen years Goodall and her associates recorded the activities of chimpanzees near Lake Tanganyika. Political unrest in the nations bordering the lake made it a dangerous area for foreigners, but the Tanzanian staff of the ethology center still observe the chimps.

Despite these long studies, chimpanzee and gorilla behavior is still not completely understood. Even greater mysteries surround the orangutan. Many more years spent watching these illusive apes will probably be needed before theories about their behavior can be proved or disproved.

Sometimes an observer, seeking a reason for an orangutan activity seen only a few times, has to settle for a good guess. There is not enough information for a definite explanation. MacKinnon reported several incidences of grooming among adult orangs during his stay in Sumatra.

He also saw males there hugging infants and, in three cases, sitting with their arms over the shoulders of females. Why does family life seem warmer among these apes than among their fellows in Borneo? Perhaps the male is needed to help protect the young from tigers and panthers, and to defend their food supply from strong, black siamangs, largest of the gibbons. There are none of these husky fruit-eaters or big cats in Borneo.

Other times the conclusions of ethologists seem to conflict. MacKinnon found more nomadic orangutans wandering through his study area than other scientists reported in theirs. However, while MacKinnon was in Borneo, heavy lumbering operations began north of Segama. Perhaps orangutans living close to this disturbance moved south to escape the invading humans and their noisy machinery.

Other ethologists thought that there were more resident orangutans in the areas they covered than MacKinnon found in his. The apes also seemed to have smaller and more stable ranges. One of these sites was on the equator and had a more constant climate with less rain than Segama. This might cause the forest to be more fruitful and able to support larger numbers of orangs. Without the seasonal influence of the monsoons, a generous supply of fruit throughout the woods might be available all year long. Animals dependent on it would not have to travel far to feed.

Other difficulties confront the ethologists who do not want to tame or touch or otherwise interfere with the orangutans they watch. While it does seem likely that the

Biruté Galdikas, with a small passenger, paddles a dugout canoe through the dense foliage of a rain forest swamp.

fully adult males father most of the baby orangutans, the active mating behavior of the sub-adults raises questions. One way to help determine the paternity of the infants would be by taking blood tests, a difficult task in field work.

Most of the scientists' studies did not last long enough to enable them to follow several generations of the slow-breeding orangutans. But in Tanjung Puting, far south in Borneo, Biruté Galdikas and her husband, Rod Brind-amour, have been observing the wild apes for five years, and plan to continue. They are making charts of orangutan family histories, which may solve the riddles about paternity. The young couple will certainly provide much more information on the wild life of these endangered animals. Knowledge of their needs could help protect them from extinction. And the study of their habits might give us clues to the early life of the more advanced primate, *Homo sapiens*.

The Travellers

AS MAWA AND UTA WANDERED THROUGH the woods they often circled and backtracked, going from one fruitful tree to another. Despite the distance they covered during the day, their nests on successive nights were often rather close.

As the mother and child roamed through their range, they began to notice unknown orangutans who appeared with growing frequency.

The new apes travelled in groups led by adult males, whose greater experience in the ways of the forest was useful in strange territory. They foraged as they went. Many wandered widely to find food, only to rejoin the troop farther along in the journey.

Where were they going? They probably did not know. They knew what they were leaving. Farther north the roar of heavy lumbering equipment had intruded on the familiar forest sounds. The orangutans moved away from the whine of saws and the repeated crashing of trees.

Although Uta had sometimes travelled with Oora for a little while, she ignored the visiting mothers from other parts of the forest. But Mawa's uneventful life was enlivened. With a series of possible playmates passing by, she even left Uta briefly to find some fun. When Mawa saw another youngster, she wrinkled her little nose and pulled her lips back in a grin, a "play face" inviting the other to frolic.

The children made the most of their short time together, punching and chasing each other. If one stopped to rest, its companion prodded until the roughhouse games began again. With gurgles and chuckles, Mawa showed her delight in the romps that spiced her placid life.

The forest was even noiser than it had been. The long calls of the male orangutans, amplified by their inflated pouches, were audible for a mile. They echoed through the woods more often. This resounding sound aided the intimidating adults in avoiding each other—and possibly fatal fights.

Now the nomads were roaming through the residents' ranges. Bubbling, rumbling, roaring warned them time and time again. One traveller, startled by a bellow from fairly close, drew erect and shook his long russet hair. He seemed to grow larger as his fur bristled and his pouch swelled beneath his wide face. He shook branches and hurled them down to the ground. He rocked his great body back and forth in widening arcs until, overbalanced, he swung down in a half-circle. Feet still clutching the branch where he had stood, he dangled head downward.

There was no response. No other orang had seen the display. After proving his power and venting his temper, the male returned to the calm pursuit of nourishment.

Later several of his troop passed through a tree where Uta rested with a branch on her head as a sun shade. Below on the forest floor, the male walked through an arch of ferns. Down the same path came the chocolate giant whom Mawa had met before. The two great apes stopped. They looked at each other.

Then, without a call or challenge, they were fighting. They bit and grappled. The chocolate orang slashed at the other's face, ripping one heavy cheek pad.

The two, locked together, fell heavily to the ground. Something cracked in the brown male's hand. Even with a broken finger, he continued the brawl.

As they wrestled, the hostile orangutans rolled across the earth in a hairy confusion of rust and chocolate. Then they struggled up and backed away from each other warily, but only for a moment. The battle began again. A strong odor of sweat rose around them. Dark flakes of forest debris stuck to their damp fur.

Finally the combatants drew apart. Still within sight of each other, they rested. The chocolate one suddenly heaved himself erect and pushed against a dead tree. The silver trunk leaned, teetered and came smashing down to earth near the russet intruder. He vanished.

Earlier, the noise had made Uta pop out from under her leafy parasol. She took one look at the ruckus and began to lead Mawa swiftly away along their familiar routes through the forest canopy. These disputes were only the concern of the males.

In Danger

THE ALIEN APES DISTURBED BY
lumbering only invaded part of the region
where John MacKinnon worked. Two study areas, which
he called A and B, provided similar habitats for the apes,
but they were separated by the Segama river. This also
divided the orangutan populations. There were approxi-
mately the same proportions of juveniles among the residents of the two areas, which suggests that at one time their
birth rates corresponded.

During MacKinnon's study, however, he found that
eight out of every ten adult females had infants in Segama
B, but only three out of ten were accompanied by very
young offspring in Segama A, which was closer to the lum-

bering. Since the proportion of infants in the A population steadily decreased, it is possible that the orangutans there changed their breeding habits in response to the disturbed conditions.

From the time a female of ten or more has her first baby, until her death at about thirty, her life is a continuing cycle of pregnancy and maternity. Since an infant demands a long period of care, companionship, nourishment and education from its mother, she waits four or five years before giving birth again. With occasional infant deaths from accident or disease, one female may only raise three or four babies successfully during her lifetime. If human activities can depress this slow breeding rate and add to the hazards of jungle life, the orangutan is indeed in danger.

Poaching is a continuing threat to the apes. Despite local laws forbidding the capture of orangutans, and international ones regulating their export and import, the estimated annual toll of orangs killed or caught in Sumatra alone is thought to be about two hundred fifty. The money to be made in illegal trade is an overwhelming temptation.

The value of an orangutan depends on its weight, up to a point. No one can handle the fully grown animals. A poacher with a fifteen-pound one-year-old can expect to receive about seventeen dollars for it, a large sum to an unemployed worker or a farmer with barren fields. The worth of the captive increases almost unendingly as it is smuggled from hand to hand. Two of the red apes were auctioned in California for $10,000 each.

A Dyak of Borneo using a sumpitan or blowgun. The trophies on his belt suggest that he has had successful hunting.

Guns are a great aide to poachers, and political unrest has put many in the hands of islanders in the Far East. But orangutans were killed long before the invention of gunpowder. Blowpipes shoot darts tipped with a mixture of poisonous tree sap and chili pepper sauce. The stinging pepper makes the ape scratch its injury, speeding the poison through its body. Even with this help by the victim, it takes three or four darts to kill an orang. One is enough for a human.

In earlier times, some tribes in Borneo were headhunters. Their members proved their manhood by taking the heads of their enemies and celebrated their success by tattooing one knuckle of their fingers for each prize they chopped from someone's neck. This practice has long been outlawed, although it was resumed briefly during World War II. Then Japanese heads were the trophies. Now the tribesmen make do with the nearest thing to human heads they can find, those of orangutans.

A tribe called the Sea Dyaks reveres the mighty apes, but this hardly helps them. A skull, watching from the rafters of a house, is believed to protect the family and home.

Deep in the rain forest there are tribes who consider roasted orangutan a delicacy. Others hope that by eating the apes they will inherit the animals' strength and courage.

These scattered customs, however, are a small danger for the orangs compared to the greatest threat, the loss of

A tribesman holds up his guardian spirit by a string passing through the orangutan's crest.

their habitat. In Borneo, wide rivers flowing through the forest simplify the removal of lumber. Wood is one of the country's greatest resources. Although the prized trees for lumber are not on the orangutan menu, falling trees tear holes in the forest. Nourishing figs, vines, ferns and flowers die. The humans sensibly reseed cutover areas with trees of value to them, but not to the apes and other forest fruit-eaters.

No one is sure how many orangutans are left. Estimates vary from less than three thousand to over ten thousand. A scientist working in Sumatra optimistically reported to the World Wildlife Fund that there were five thousand red apes there in 1975. Then, less optimistically, he predicted that half of these would lose their habitat in the next ten to fifteen years.

In Sumatra, forests are felled for land as well as lumber. The island is more densely populated than Borneo. Farmers living near the woods cut and burn them to clear the earth for crops of rice and maize. But in this mountainous terrain, repeated storms erode the ground no longer protected by a compact cloak of trees and undergrowth.

The lush rain forests actually grow in poor, claylike soil. The plants have shallow roots that quickly suck up the minerals provided by fallen leaves and other decaying matter. This rapid recycling of nutrients in a closed system—from tree to earth to tree—means that deep carpets of enriching humus never accumulate as they do in our deciduous woods. When the ground of the rain forest is exposed, tropical downpours promptly wash out what little nourish-

Genap Amansar, poling the boat in the stern, was once a very able orangutan hunter. He now uses his woodsman's skills to rescue apes caught by poachers and to retrain them in the natural ways of forest life.

ment it contains. The tropical sun bakes the clay brick hard.

Soon only poorer crops can be grown in the dense, depleted soil. Then shrubs and bushes take over. Even these are cut every few years to provide grazing land for cattle and domestic buffalo.

Most of the Sumatran orangutans live in the Gunung Leuser Reserve, an area of deep, stream-cut valleys, high mountains and tumultuous waterfalls. It will never be completely tamed by humans. However, the Reserve is unfortunately reserved for the extraction of lumber, not the protection of animal life. Much of it is vulnerable to the insatiable saws and the encroaching farmers who live on its borders.

When the riches of the forest run out, new sources of

income will have to be found and new methods of agriculture adopted. It would be best if people could learn to change their ways even before they are forced to by their own destructive habits.

The preservation of the Gunung Leuser Reserve would benefit not only the disappearing orang but also other endangered animals, including the almost-extinct Sumatran rhinoceros. Most parts of the rhino are believed to have medical or religious powers, but the horn is the most highly prized. Just one can fetch a price of $1,000 or more. As a result, by 1970 there were only about fifty-eight of the animals in Sumatra and less than a hundred in Borneo.

Virgin rain forests are falling at a rate of fifty acres each minute. This slaughter not only deprives orangs, rhinos and countless other wild creatures of their homes, but also greatly diminishes the resources of the earth. Coffee, cacao and rubber plants were all developed from tropical ancestors. L-dopa, used to treat victims of Parkinson's disease, comes from the seeds of a jungle vine. But if the wealth of the rain forests is measured only by the lumber in them, many more foods, medicines, pesticides and other valuable products will never even be discovered.

Vegetation extracts carbon dioxide from the air, replacing it with oxygen, and the giant rain forests do a large part of this "breathing" for the entire earth. It has also been predicted that disastrous changes in climate would follow the loss of the broad green belt of tropical jungles that circles the globe at the equator. Orangutans need the rain forests. So do we.

The Death

THE RESTLESS CALLING OF THE MALE orangutans tapered off after the strangers left the residents' ranges to find new homes deeper in the forest.

When the worst of the January rains had passed, it was nine months since Uta had been courted by the chocolate male. She gave birth to a baby, and Mawa, as her fourth birthday drew near, found herself banished from her mother's nest.

But the growing youngster stayed by Uta as she travelled and foraged with the tiny infant securely at her side. At night Mawa nested close to the other two. The baby fascinated his older sister.

Mawa watched as Uta cleaned little Rang's long bronze

hair with her teeth and nibbled at his fingernails to shorten them. Once, on the ground, the mother put the tiny tot down on his belly. He flailed his scrawny arms and legs in a vain attempt to crawl. When Uta offered him one long finger, Rang grasped it tightly. His mother gently pulled him across the earth. Up in the trees Uta sometimes held her son firmly around his tummy with one large hand while the other put slim vines into his hands and feet. Rang's education had begun.

Mawa's lessons in motherhood had started, too. She not only saw all that Uta did with her baby, but she was allowed to play with him. Rang squirmed with pleasure when Mawa tickled him. He squeezed his sister's fingers with his wrinkled little hand as eagerly as he clutched his mother's fur.

One day in April Mawa and Uta were stripping leaves from lianas hurriedly. They were working fast to fill their bellies with this food, not their favorite, but the most abundant at the time. A storm was driving in, pushing sullen clouds across the sky.

Perhaps Uta was in too much of a hurry. She did not notice a man moving silently towards her until the shot. Unhurt but terrified, the orangutan worked her way back into the tangle of vines. Slowed by the clinging Rang, she did not flee, but tried to hide in the depths of the foliage.

The quicker Mawa sped to the top of the tree. A clouded leopard, who had followed the orang family, hoping to catch little Rang in an unguarded instant, also ran away. The medium-sized cat feared the greatest predator of all.

If an orangutan cannot frighten an enemy with its noisy

threats, it will often remain hidden and still for hours to escape danger. But Uta did not succeed. The hunter had seen her leafy refuge. Shot after shot tore through the flimsy foliage to hit the red ape. Finally she tumbled from the tree.

As the man wrested Rang from his mother's body, he objected with his toothless gums and all his feeble strength. But once in the hunter's arms, instinctively, desperately, the infant ape clung to him.

The man was dismayed with his tiny captive, only a month old. He had expected a stronger baby. Now he hoped that his wife could care for such a young one. Pet orangutans brought prestige. If he gave it to one of the village leaders, he could expect favors in return. Maybe he should just sell it. The orang would bring a good price once it had fattened up on large helpings of rice.

The storm burst swiftly, hurling rain at the earth. The hunter decided to get the baby home before counting his profits. He pulled his shirt over the infant, but it was soaked immediately and stuck to Rang's auburn fur and his captor's back, wrapping them together in clammy cloth.

Rain poured over Uta's body, protecting it briefly from the jungle scavengers that would feast for days on such a find. The mother ape's long hair floated in the puddles growing around her. Her pelt was flecked with petals washed down by the storm, soft white flakes on deep chestnut.

After raising Oora, Tan, Mawa, and for a short while, Rang, the solitary ape was alone again.

High in the tree, the orphaned Mawa sheltered under a

broad branch, whimpering. When the rain stopped, she would move off into the forest. Although she might follow Oora and her baby now and then, or join another adolescent, she was beginning her independent life. After many years she would have her own children, if she survived.

Orphans Adopted

T OM HARRISSON GAVE HIS WIFE, Barbara, an unusual present for Christmas in 1958—a baby orangutan. She named the fifteen-pound bundle of red fur "Bob."

Bob was really more of an obligation than a gift. Since it is illegal to keep captive orangutans in Borneo, the year-old ape had been confiscated by Forest Guards from a villager. What should be done with him? The Guards decided it would be best to hand the baby over to Tom Harrisson, who was the curator of the Sarawak Museum in Kuching.

The Harrissons enclosed a small porch outside their bathroom with wire and equipped it with ropes, shelves, a swing and a bed. There Bob could both romp in his cage and peer through the window at the fascinating morning rituals of his new parents.

Bob was not an only child for long. Undernourished Eve arrived soon after, weighing only seven pounds. Her neck was sore from the chain that had tied her beneath a Chinese trader's house. She had been fed only bananas and biscuits and refused to drink milk until Bidai, a patient youth hired to help with the orphans, gave it to her in a spoon. Bidai cuddled the little ape and played with her until she became very dependent on him and thoroughly spoiled.

Then came Tony, Frank and Bill. Tiny Tony was a sick skeleton covered with boils and suffering from pneumonia and worms. Although less than a year old, he had lost even the instinct to cling. He curled up alone with his miseries and very soon died.

Bill had been found by a Guard sitting in the forest next to the decomposing body of his mother. Frank and he were both still infants. They slept together in the same sack at night and complained loudly if they were separated. Eve, by then a jealous two-year-old, objected to any attention her friend Bidai gave to the new babies.

Eventually Barbara Harrisson left her three children briefly and went on an expedition into the rain forest to watch the wild orangutans. She felt that more knowledge of their natural lives might help her take better care of her growing family.

The sight of these orangs at home in the treetops con-

Patient Bidai with his devoted and dependent friend, Eve.

vinced Barbara Harrisson that she should become more of
an "ape mother" and less of a human one. Bidai, instead of
romping on the lawn with the babies during their exercise
times, put them up in the garden trees. Frank and Bill ate
leaves and fruit and played happily there. Eve was not
attracted to this boisterous life. Bidai had to go aloft himself and sit on branches for hours to tempt her to join them.

Although Barbara Harrisson dreamed of returning the
babies to life in the wild, this proved to be impossible.

They had stayed with humans too long and were too dependent on affection and abundant food. Reluctantly, the Harrissons sent Bob, Eve and Bill to zoos while they were still young enough to adapt, zoos chosen with great care.

Then Nigel arrived to keep the remaining Frank company. After avoiding trees for several days, Nigel suddenly began to stay out overnight in them. He built nests and even let Frank help him. Frank's aid usually meant taking apart whatever Nigel had put together.

When the garden trees grew ragged and their fruit was exhausted, a kindly neighbor allowed the apes to visit his property. Barbara Harrisson drove them to their afternoon outings. One rainy day, worried about their welfare, she arrived early to take them home. They were perfectly happy, up in a tree. The orangs were snuggled on either side of Bidai, all three protected by his umbrella.

The next arrival was a real infant, five-pound four-month Ossy. Barbara Harrisson made him a bed in a basket with a bar overhead to clutch. It was decorated daily with fresh flowers and leaves to keep the baby busy playing and tasting.

When Janie joined the family, her ten teeth told the Harrissons that she was four months older than the toothless Ossy, but she weighed the same. She had lived on bananas, was infested with hookworms and had a broken arm. Like Tony, she soon died. Too much had happened to these two infant orangs in their short lives.

By winter, a teasing, destructive Nigel was almost too strong to handle. And time was running out. The Harris-

The infant Ossy, respectably clothed in a towel diaper, fits comfortably in a human hand.

sons were going to England soon on leave. They had to take their apes with them to new homes in zoos.

Just before she sailed, Barbara Harrisson received another baby, Derek. He joined little Ossy in one cage while a larger and sturdier structure held the older orangs. For most of the seven-week trip, the cages stayed on the ship's deck. When the weather was fine, the apes were let out for exercise, supervised by Barbara Harrisson. Her care kept them alive and healthy during the warm days at the beginning of the trip and the stormy ones in colder climates, when room was made for the animals below deck.

It was his sense of humor that probably kept the captain alive and well despite the experiments of the older orangs. Outdoors, they discovered and dismantled the lifeboats' emergency equipment. Inside, they ripped heating pipes from the walls. Whenever he could, Frank escaped to the crew's shower, where he hid in a stall, waiting patiently for a cooperative sailor to turn on the water.

When the Harrissons returned to Borneo, new apes came into their lives, and at last they had a chance to try returning the orphans to the wild. The government let them release confiscated orangutans in the Bako Reservation and Park near Kuching. Twice a day local helpers fed their guests, including the two adolescents, Arthur and Cynthia. At all times the orangs were supposed to be free to join their forest cousins, but the experiment failed. There were no wild red apes in the Reservation, which had few fruiting trees.

However, an idea had been born. In 1964 the government set up a halfway house to introduce once captive orangutans to their natural ways. This Sabah Orangutan Rehabilitation Center was farther north in Borneo, near Sepilok, in a ten thousand acre virgin forest populated by wild apes.

Under the direction of the Assistant Chief Game Warden, Stanley de Silva, fifty-one orangutans have been at the center. Some have died, including Arthur from Bako. He had grown into a violent unreliable adult who had to be destroyed to save the rangers from his attacks.

Cynthia was also moved to Sepilok. She was among the eight apes who continued to stay near their human helpers. During the first nine years, all the other survivors graduated to the forest.

Cynthia's long life as a captive robbed her of any independence. Other orangutans were also influenced by their earlier experiences. Henry came from a lumber camp where he had been taught obscene gestures to amuse the workers. Winnie was a tobacco addict. She threw herself at anyone smoking, biting and struggling in her desperate attempts to snatch a cigarette.

Some of the orangutans alternated life in the wild with the comforts of the center. Joan came and went, and then produced wobbly little Joanne in 1967, fathered by a wild ape. Four years later, Joan was no longer accompanied by her daughter. No one knows whether she died or whether she is still roaming the jungle freely. But her mother found another suitor in the forest, and brought her second infant, Johnnie, to visit in 1972.

Joan returns to visit Sepilok with Johnnie, her second baby fathered by a wild orangutan.

Halfway Houses

THE IDEA OF REPATRIATING CAP-
tive apes eventually spread to Sumatra. Ans
Rijksen-Graatsma and her veterinarian husband, Herman
D. Rijksen, set up the first halfway house in the Gunung
Leuser Reserve there in 1971. The station was near Ke-
tambe in a remote area of the forest, surrounded by rivers
that would limit the orangutans' wandering.

Two years later another refuge was opened in a different region of the Reserve near Bohorok. It was run by two
young Swiss women, Monica Borner-Loewensberg and
Regina Frey. In addition to nursing orphaned orangutans
back to health and a natural life, the staff at both stations
carried out scientific studies of the wild red apes in the
areas.

At the reservations, the first stops for the orangutan guests were quarantine cages. Here they were kept for two or three weeks while they were examined for diseases and dewormed. Because most of the apes were undernourished and weak, if not actually sick, they were very susceptible to infection. Since orangutans can acquire human diseases, including tuberculosis, polio, malaria and encephalitis, the orphans were given vaccinations to protect them from the ailments of the workers who cared for them. Without this preventative treatment, the station orangs could become carriers and introduce alien diseases to the wild population when they went into the forests.

Many of the captive orangs brought to the stations had lived under dreadful conditions. One had spent six years in a cage just a little larger than one cubic yard. After a similar long spell in a small cage, another, Simi, was imprisoned in the empty engine space of a truck for several more years. She was fed through a little hole in the hood.

A young female, Tjali, had been the constant companion of her American "father," accompanying him to bars every evening. Tjali was an alcoholic. Gareng, tied to the ground by a short chain for three of his eight years, had been crippled by inactivity and malnutrition.

When the orangutans had passed their physicals, they were moved from the quarantine areas to cages deeper in the forest. The doors were open during the day. At night the adolescent apes usually nested in nearby trees, while the little ones were locked in to protect them from predators.

Ans Rijksen-Graatsma feeding a new arrival, Bumi, who was so emaciated that he gained more than two pounds a week at first. In addition to the wound in the center of his forehead, Bumi had cuts around his neck made by a tight wire collar.

Bananas were distributed daily to all the orphans, but only bananas. Orangutans are the gourmets of the jungle, which provides them with at least two hundred varieties of food. The repetitive diet at the stations encouraged them to forage in the wild for more interesting fare.

At Bohorok, with at least twenty apes at the station or roaming freely near it, the afternoon feeding parties were lively ones. Occasionally a wild orang would sneak among its tame cousins, grab as many bananas as it could carry in its mouth and one hand and then race away with the loot.

Milk was meant only for the babies, but older apes sometimes managed to steal a drink in the turmoil. A deprived infant would roll away from the heaving mass of red fur to stage a private temper tantrum, beating its head and screaming in frustration.

Either Frey or Borner-Loewensberg always attended the parties. This gave them a chance to see how the graduates of the station who spent most of their time in the woods were getting along. After the banana supply ran out and the roaming orangutans had returned to the forest, the hostess romped with the little ones left behind, still too young to be on their own. Then it was bedtime and the babies were tucked into the cages, usually by twos and always with leafy branches to use building practice nests.

Some of the babies needed climbing lessons. The first reaction of an inexperienced infant, when lifted from the firm ground and placed in a stand of waving bamboo, was sheer shrieking terror. But, in spite of such fears, the animal had to learn that it was an arboreal ape.

On the left, a wild female orangutan hopefully keeps her eyes on the bananas held by Seun, but the food is meant for Bujong, the rehabilitant sub-adult male in the center.

People at the stations tried not to play with, or even touch, the older orangs, to help them lose their trust in humans. That was hard to do with Doli. She had been raised as a much-loved child and considered humans as proper parents and playmates. Doli was the only orphan to wander back to the house and pester tourists.

Despite her happy life with people, Doli was overjoyed when she was first freed. She hurled herself through the trees with abandon—until she fell and broke her arm. After it healed, a wiser ape climbed with care.

Another little orang, Olib, also had trouble with trees. After he had been missing twenty-four hours, his constant companion, Purba, led people to his fallen friend. Olib had a broken jaw. He was taken to the hospital on a rubber plantation to have the bones clipped together. A pet dog must be anesthetized even to have its teeth cleaned, but this amiable and gentle orangutan, wide awake, let the strange doctor probe his mouth without a nip.

Many of the orangutans who passed through the stations came and went between wilderness and civilization, joined at times by forest apes who dared to visit the humans. Other orangs, after learning how to survive in the woods, took to the jungle permanently—some independently, some helped by a piggyback ride, a boat trip or a helicopter flight. Among these was a vicious female, one of the very few apes to show hostility to humans despite the maltreatment many had suffered. She was taken so deep into the forest that she would always be safe from people—and they from her.

Usually the orangutans who left the station voluntarily

The Rijksens with four of their charges. Ans is wearing a shirt decorated with a panda, the symbol of the World Wildlife Fund, and with the Dutch name of the international organization.

were adolescents or adults. But sometimes babies attached themselves to larger friends and returned to the woods with them. Most of the older females chosen as substitute mothers accepted their roles with all that they implied— tutor, transporter, playmate and warm, red security blanket. Little orphans without foster mothers hugged each other for comfort or held their own hands with their toes.

Some of the apes, however, could never leave the stations. One at Bohorok had been caged in a small box for so long that she had become mentally incompetent. She was unable to live on her own.

Rescuing captive orangs from their too-often tortured lives was important for those individuals, but returning a hundred or more specimens to the wild will not save the species. The halfway houses, however, did give the government places to put confiscated orangutans. This meant that laws against poaching and private possession of orangutans, first passed in 1931, could finally be enforced.

The rehabilitation efforts also dramatized the plight of the orangs, although misunderstandings did occur. Some Indonesians decided that raising the orphans was a hobby of the odd Europeans. The more apes they had the happier they would be. Such well-meaning people had to be persuaded not to hunt for even more babies to please the foreigners.

Visitors from other countries had always found the red apes amusing pets and companions for their children. They not only paid money for the animals, but set a bad example. If the rich, powerful foreigners prized such pets, the local people wanted them, too. The orangutan was a status symbol.

Apes still held by poachers were easy to confiscate. Those that belonged to more important people presented problems. The owners had to be convinced, tactfully, that their pets would be better off back in the forest. Some were approached for a year before giving up their animals.

Tourists brought other problems. Many were not content to watch the half-tame orangs. They wanted their pictures taken with the "fiercest" one available. This thwarted attempts to make the apes less used to humans and increased their exposure to disease.

However, foreign tourists brought money much needed in Sumatra. And visits by curious local people enabled the staffs to explain why the orangs should not be molested and how essential undisturbed rain forests were for them. The stations' educational efforts might be their greatest contribution to the species' survival.

At Bohorok they are planning a travelling exhibit financed by the World Wildlife Fund. Slides and motion pictures on conservation themes will be shown in schools and villages to teach the laws and the reasons for them. Then people may understand that the orangutan is more valuable as a wild red ape than as a pet, a gift or a source of illegal income.

House Wreckers

B IRUTÉ GALDIKAS'S AMBITION TO study orangutans was encouraged by the late Dr. Louis Leakey, an anthropologist renowned for the early fossils of ancient people he discovered in Africa. Leakey was interested in the great apes because knowledge of their behavior might increase our understanding of prehistoric humans. Years before, the persuasive doctor had already convinced Jane Goodall to study chimpanzees and Dian Fossey, gorillas.

Galdikas was working on a graduate degree in anthropology under Leakey's supervision when she decided to go to the rain forests of Borneo. She was accompanied by her husband, Rod Brindamour, whose technical skills, photographic ability and experience in the forests of Canada proved invaluable.

A project like the field study of orangutans costs money, often more than can be provided by a single source. The results may be of interest to many countries. The grants received by Galdikas show the complexity of financing scientific research and its international character today. Funds were given by the Leakey Foundation of Los Angeles, four other foundations including one in the Netherlands, the New York Zoological Society and the National Geographic Society of Washington, D.C. The work was sponsored by the Indonesian Institute of Sciences and the Nature Protection and Wildlife Management Service.

Since 1971 the Galdikas-Brindamours have been following orangutans in fourteen square miles of the Tanjung Puting Reserve. They have logged seven thousand hours of observations. The couple, burdened with binoculars, and sometimes cameras and tape recorders, travels on eighty miles of trails hacked through the swampy jungle. Cracking twigs, thrashing foliage or falling pits and pieces of fruit alert them to the presence of the apes. Galdikas has followed some for days, leaving them after they retired, and then walking miles before dawn the next morning to reach the nests before their occupants arose.

The Galdikas-Brindamours watched the first desperate fight between two adult males seen by scientists. They also noted that, contrary to the arboreal reputation of the species, these heavy senior citizens do almost all of their long-distance travelling on the ground. Three nests on

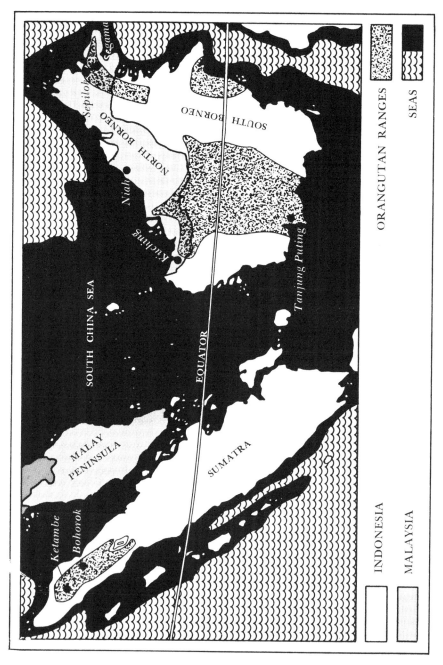

A map showing the rescue and research areas in Sumatra
(Indonesia) and Borneo (Indonesia and Malaysia).

fallen logs were found, the first wild ones recorded so low.

The Galdikas-Brindamours have learned to recognize over forty orangutans that they meet on their patrols. They have been able to "habituate" some of these, making the animals so used to them that the apes ignore the scientists and go on with their natural activities. For more than three years they tracked fully grown Nick for as long as thirteen hours a day. He finally became totally habituated.

At first Nick fled on elevated highways through the canopy as soon as he saw humans. He learned later that it was safe to come down to the ground to search for insects, but his hunting always led him away from the observers. Then, after actually approaching the Galdikas-Brinda-mours while looking for termites in rotten logs, Nick sat down calmly within fifteen feet of them to enjoy his snack.

Two Indonesian biology students have joined the con-tinuing studies of the red apes' ranges, foods, social behav-ior and family trees. The students also help look after orphaned orangutans. Shortly after the Galdikas-Brind-amours began their project, the Indonesian government asked them to care for apes confiscated from illegal owners. Their jungle camp became a rehabilitation center for the orangs.

Among the first arrivals was Akmad. She was fairly in-dependent and slept in the trees around the camp at night. But Subiarso, Rio and Sugito preferred the shelter of the Galdikas-Brindamour's hut. There they spent the night on the floor in cozy nests made of old clothes and sacks.

One-year-old Sugito had been kept in an orange crate

Sugito asleep, snugly nestled in an old dress of Galdikas and topped by the khaki hat she always wears in the field. Apes and other animals who cannot change their own appearance become habituated more easily if the scientists watching them use the same clothing from day to day.

when he should have been close to his mother. Nevertheless, his instincts were normal, and he immediately adopted Galdikas, hanging from her side wherever she went. He screeched if she tried to switch his position and became hysterical when she wanted to change her clothes. This had its advantages, however. As an orangutan "mother," with Sugito and sometimes other red babies clinging to her, the young scientist was accepted more readily by the wild apes she followed.

An Indonesian woman who had raised an orangutan, Cempaka, for seven years was finally persuaded to surrender her beloved pet to the center. The sixty-two pound "baby" had grown almost as large as her frail foster mother. Cempaka was a thoroughly domesticated lady. She rinsed and wrung rags in buckets of soapy water, used forks and spoons at mealtimes and cooked, mixing flour, sugar and eggs and then stirring her batter vigorously.

The spoiled ape soon found her way to the Galdikas-Brindamour's bed—both for company and for the tasty kapok seeds she found when she ripped the mattress apart. Orangutans are hard to discipline. Because of their lonely life, they do not have to consider the needs of others. When Cempaka moved into bed, what little order had remained in the hut disappeared. Why should Rio, Subiarso and Sugito sleep on the floor?

Even the independent Akmad found the crowded bed a welcome shelter on rainy nights. To check on the weather, she thrust her head through the thatched roof now and then. If a downpour continued, she went back to sleep, ignoring the water streaming through her observation holes on people and apes alike.

The orangutans took over the human habitation with gusto. They decorated everything with their toothmarks. Baby-proof medicine bottles were apes'-play for them to open. Toothpaste and glue, delicious. Disorganizing scientific papers and dismantling photographic equipment amused the orangs. They made nests out of books, clothing, mosquito netting and even an umbrella.

Rio joined Cempaka in sucking the ink out of pens. Candles and flashlight bulbs were added to the orang diet, but still the apes thrived. They hid flashlight batteries in their immense mouths. An adolescent orangutan was once seen with five bananas in her mouth. Three batteries were no problem for a younger one.

The orphans arranged things according to strange schemes of their own. Cempaka flavored the morning coffee by emptying bowls of salt into it. Sometimes she spiced the brew with a dirty sock or two. Sugito hid rice in his capacious mouth until he found a chance to deposit it into his foster mother's cup. Milk was also great fun to spit or spray at other orangutans.

At suppertime Galdikas was surrounded by eager eyes. While she defended her noodles from attacks on one side, a little arm sneaked in from the other to grab a snarly handful. A firm "Mine!" directed at a coffee-loving ape on the

Rod Brindamour, the other half of the team engaged in studying and saving orangutans, giving Cempaka a snack.

Sugito offers his foster mother a kiss.

right, gave one on the left a chance to steal a sip. And then apologize with a funnel-mouthed kiss.

One time, after Sugito took the last bit on her plate, Galdikas complained to him that he was just not being fair. Rod Brindamour, who was not considered an orangutan "mother" by the orphans, was free from harassment. Unsympathetically, he suggested to his wife that she learn to eat more quickly.

In 1974 the ape-assaulted couple built a solid wooden house with walls. They moved in even before there were any screens, sure that the height of the windows would protect their privacy. The deserted Sugito, screaming his objections, leaned a stick through one open window in a matter of minutes and scrambled up it. The Galdikas-Brindamours did not live in peace until all the screens were installed.

The rickety huts were left as a playground. It did not take the busy apes long to reduce them to a complete shambles. Then they had to nest in trees like proper orangutans.

Would the rehabilitated orphans ever become normal animals of the forest, or would they be affected too much by their early years with humans? Some orangs, after watching the tool-using people, dug in the ground with sticks. One attacked a snake with a branch, and Cempaka was as adept at manipulating sticks as she was at using a spoon.

Since people often took the orphans' hands and led them across the ground, the tame orangs became accustomed to walking erect more often than wild ones do.

The apes were bright enough to appreciate their easy life. Some shunned the hardships of an uncivilized existence. Even if they wanted to give up bananas for more varied natural foods, they found it hard to leave the people who had cared for them. The orphans also developed strong attachments to their orangutan companions.

Can these social, bipedal, stick-wielding apes introduce new habits to the wild populations? Galdikas doubts it. All young orangs enjoy company, whether they live in refuges, zoos, labs or the forest. The change in character of older apes is probably due to inevitable physical developments. Galdikas thinks it likely that, whether they grew up swinging on bars, beds or vines, hormonal and other bodily changes urge all orangutans into a lonely life as they mature.

Farewell

THE REAL THREAT FACED BY ALL
the orangutans, rehabilitated and wild, comes
from humans hungry for their forests.

Words spoken over a century ago by Chief Seattle in
answer to a request that his tribe move to a reservation
are still valid today, if "white man" is changed to "humanity."

"We know the white man . . . does not care. . . . He
treats his mother, the earth, and his brother, the sky, as
things to be bought, plundered, sold like sheep or bright
beads. His appetite will devour the earth and leave behind
only a desert. . . .

"What is man without the beasts? If all the beasts were

gone, man would die from a great loneliness of spirit. For whatever happens to the beasts soon happens to man. All things are connected. . . .

"Whatever befalls the earth befalls the sons of the earth. Man did not weave the web of life: he is merely a strand in it. Whatever he does to the web, he does to himself."

Extinct races of humans died out because they could not compete with more successful ones. Our intelligence has taken us to the moon. Are we also wise enough to share the earth with the beasts—the great apes among them? Or will *Homo sapiens* murder its nearest relatives again?

•

Endangered species include the great apes—gorilla, chimpanzee and orangutan—and us.

NOTES ON SOURCES

In the story of Mawa, the description of orangutan life is based on *In Search of the Red Apes,* by John MacKinnon; "Orangutans, Indonesia's 'People of the Forest,' " by Biruté Galdikas; the scientific papers on their field studies by Davenport, Horr, MacKinnon, Rijksen and Rodman; and telephone conversations and correspondence with Galdikas. Statistics on the types of food eaten by the orangutans and the amount of rainfall at different times come from MacKinnon's article in *Animal Behaviour.* Numerous sources supplied the background information on the Borneo rain forests and their flora and fauna.

25 "Yet regard . . . Ourang outang." From *Historiae Naturalis,* 1658, by Jacob Bontius; as reprinted in Yerkes, *The Great Apes.*

26, 27 "Intermediate link" and "chain of creation." From *Orang-Outang, sive Homo Sylvestris; or, the Anatomy of a Pygmie compared with that of a monkey, an ape, and a man,* 1699, by Edward Tyson; as reprinted in Reynolds, *The Apes.*

32 "The Monkeys, Apes . . . that offend them." From *A Voyage to and from the island of Borneo,"* 1714, by Daniel Beeckman; as reprinted in Harrisson, *Orang-utan.*

33, 34 "This Orang-outang or Pongo . . . of his nature." From *Histoire naturelle, générale et particulière,* 1749–1767, by the Comte de Buffon; as reprinted in Harrisson; *Orang-utan.*

34 "Of a melancholy appearance" and

34 "During its state of liberty . . . proper manner." From *Description de l'espèce de singe aussi singulier que très rare, nommé orang-utang, de l'île de Borneo,* 1778, by Arnout Vosmaer; as reprinted in Goodrich, *The Animal Kingdom Illustrated.*

37 "The general impression is . . . to trace." From *Naturalist's Library,* 1833.

42 "They drink from a glass . . . to wine." From *Annales du Muséum d'Histoire Naturelle,* Vol. 15, by the Baron de Cuvier; as reprinted in Menault, *Wonders of Animal Instinct.*

45 "His mildness . . . teased him." "Might often be seen . . . human nature." and

146

45, 46 "So difficult . . . human posture." From *Narrative of a Journey in the interior of China,*" 1818, by Clarke Abel; as reprinted in *Naturalist's Library.*

46 "Accompanied by . . . how to observe." From *Wonders of Animal Instinct,* late 19th century, by Ernest Menault.

51 "Of an agility . . . from humanity." From *Tales of Mystery and Imagination,* 1935, by Edgar Allan Poe.

55 "You will see . . . as my baby." By Alfred Russel Wallace; as reprinted in Sanderson, *Ivan Sanderson's Book of Great Jungles.*

55, 56 "One of these we shot and killed . . . to get it." From *The Malay Archipelago,* 1869, by Alfred Russel Wallace.

56 "Would not have exchanged . . . the whole season through." By William T. Hornaday; as reprinted in Bourne, *Primate Oddysey.*

75 "To an Orang . . . natural jokes." By Tom Harrisson, in the preface to *Orang-utan,* 1963, by Barbara Harrisson.

93*ff* Chapter Twenty, "In the Field," is based on the field studies of Davenport, Galdikas, Horr, MacKinnon, Rijksen and Rodman.

143 From the speech of Chief Seattle addressed to President Franklin Pierce, 1854; as reprinted in *Wildlife,* March, 1976.

Suggestions for Further Reading

ABOUT ORANG PENDEK

Grumley, Michael. *There Are Giants in the Earth.* New York: Doubleday & Company, Inc., 1974.

Heuvelmans, Bernard. *On the Track of Unknown Animals.* Translated from the French by Richard Garnett. New York: Hill & Wang, 1958.

Napier, John. *Bigfoot: The Yeti and Sasquatch in Myth and Reality.* New York: E. P. Dutton & Company, Inc., 1973.

ABOUT ORANGUTANS

Galdikas, Biruté. "Orangutans, Indonesia's 'People of the Forest.'" *National Geographic Magazine.* Washington: National Geographic Society, October, 1975.

Harrisson, Barbara. *Orang-utan.* New York: Doubleday & Company, Inc., 1963.

MacKinnon, John. *In Search of the Red Ape.* New York: Holt, Rinehart & Winston, 1974.

MacKinnon, John and the Editors of Time–Life Books. *Borneo*. Amsterdam: Time–Life International, 1975.

ABOUT THE GREAT APES

Bourne, Geoffrey H. *Primate Odyssey*. New York: G. P. Putnam's Sons, 1974.

Goodall, Jane. *In the Shadow of Man*. Boston: Houghton Mifflin Company, 1971. (In paperback, New York: Dell Publishing Company, Inc., 1972.)

Gray, Robert. *The Great Apes: The Natural Life of Chimpanzees, Gorillas, Orangutans and Gibbons*. New York: W. W. Norton & Company, Inc., 1969.

Kay, Helen. *Apes*. New York: The Macmillan Company, 1970.

Kevles, Bettyann. *Watching the Wild Apes: The Primate Studies of Goodall, Fossey and Galdikas*. New York: E. P. Dutton & Company, Inc., 1976.

Reynolds, Vernon. *The Apes: The Gorilla, Chimpanzee, Orangutan and Gibbon—their History and their World*. New York: E. P. Dutton & Company, 1967.

Schaller, George B. *The Year of the Gorilla*. Chicago: University of Chicago Press, 1963.

Bibliography

Attenborough, David. "To Borneo with Attenborough." *Animals Magazine.* London: Nigel Sitwell, Ltd., November, 1973.

Bourne, Geoffrey H. *Primate Odyssey.* New York: G. P. Putnam's Sons, 1974.

—*The Ape People.* New York: G. P. Putnam's Sons, 1971.

Bridges, William. *Gathering of Animals: An Unconventional History of the New York Zoological Society.* New York: Harper & Row, 1974.

Chief Seattle. "A Chief's Lament." *Wildlife Magazine.* London: Wildlife Publications, Ltd., March, 1976.

Colbert, Edwin H. *Wandering Lands and Animals.* New York: E. P. Dutton & Company, Inc., 1973.

Curry-Lindahl, Kai. *Let Them Live: A Worldwide Survey of Animals Threatened with Extinction.* New York: William Morrow & Company, Inc., 1972.

Davenport, Richard K. "The Orang-utan in Sabah." *Folia Primatologica,* Vol. 5. New York: New York Zoological Society, 1967.

Figuier, Louis. *Mammalia: Their Various Orders and Habits.* New York: D. Appleton & Company, 1870.

Fisher, James; Simon, Noel and Vincent, Jack. *Wildlife in Danger.* New York: The Viking Press, 1969.

Frey, Regina. "Sumatra's Red Apes Return to the Wild." *Wildlife Magazine.* London: Wildlife Publications, Ltd., August, 1975.

Galdikas, Biruté. "Orangutans, Indonesia's 'People of the Forest.' " *National Geographic Magazine.* Washington: National Geographic Society, October, 1975.

Goodrich, S. C. *The Animal Kingdom Illustrated,* Vol. 1. New York: A. J. Johnson, 1872.

Gray, Robert. *The Great Apes: The Natural Life of Chimpanzees, Gorillas, Orangutans and Gibbons.* New York: W. W. Norton & Company, Inc., 1969.

Gwynne, Peter. "Doomed Jungles?" *International Wildlife.* Washington: National Wildlife Federation, July-August, 1976.

"Half Surviving Orang-utans in Sumatra Doomed to Lose Habitat." *Press Release No. 34.* Morges, Switzerland: The World Wildlife Fund, October 10, 1975.

Harrisson, Barbara. *Orang-utan.* New York: Doubleday & Company, Inc., 1963.

—"Research on Orang-utan Ecology by Biruté Galdikas-Brindamour." *Borneo Research Bulletin,* Vol. 5, No. 1. West Lafayette, Indiana: Purdue University, April, 1973.

Harrisson, Tom. "Orang-utan." *Animal Life 1973: The World Conservation Yearbook.* Edited by Nigel Sitwell. Danbury, Connecticut: The Danbury Press, 1973.

Heuvelmans, Bernard. *On the Track of Unknown Animals.* Translated from the French by Richard Garnett. New York: Hill & Wang, 1958.

Hornaday, William T. *Two Years in the Jungle.* New York: Charles Scribner's Sons, 1885.

Horr, David Agee. "Orang-utan Watching: A Day in the Life . . ." *Borneo Research Bulletin,* Vol. 5, No. 1. West Lafayette, Indiana: Purdue University, April, 1973.

—"Our Red-Haired Kin of the Rain Forest." *Life.* New York: Time Inc., March 28, 1969.

—"The Borneo Orang-utan: Population Structure and Dynamics in Relationship to Ecology and Reproductive Strategy." *Primate Behavior: Developments in Field and Laboratory Research,* Vol. 4. Edited by Leonard A. Rosenblum. New York: Academic Press, 1975.

"In Search of the Great Apes." Television program. Washington: National Geographic Society, January, 1975.

Kevles, Bettyann. *Watching the Wild Apes: The Primate Studies of Goodall, Fossey and Galdikas.* New York: E. P. Dutton & Company, Inc., 1976.

Ley, Willy. *Dawn of Zoology.* Englewood Cliffs, New Jersey: Prentice-Hall, Inc., 1968.

Linden, Eugene. *Apes, Men and Language.* New York: Saturday Review Press, E. P. Dutton & Company, Inc., 1974.

Livingston, Bernard. *Zoo: Animals, People, Places.* New York: Arbor House, 1974.

MacKinnon, John. "Behavior and Ecology of Orang-utans." *Animal Behaviour,* Vol. 22, No. 1. London: Baillière Tindall, 1974.

—*In Search of the Red Ape.* New York: Holt, Rinehart & Winston, 1974.

MacKinnon, John and the Editors of Time–Life Books. *Borneo.* Amsterdam: The World's Wild Places/Time–Life International, 1975.

Martin, Jo. "Monkeyshines at the Zoo." *Daily News.* New York: New York News, April 14, 1972.

Menault, Ernest. *Wonders of Animal Instinct.* Translated from the French. New York: Cassell, Petter and Galpin, late 19th century.

Mydans, Carl. "Orangutans Can Return to the Wild with Some Help." *Smithsonian.* Washington: Smithsonian Associates, November, 1973.

Napier, John. *Bigfoot: The Yeti and Sasquatch in Myth and Reality.* New York: E. P. Dutton & Company, Inc., 1973.

Naturalist's Library, Mammalia: Monkeys. Edited by Sir William Jardine. Edinburgh: W. H. Lizars, 1833.

"Orang-Utan." *Red Data Book, Mammalia,* Vol. 1. Morges, Switzerland: International Union for Conservation of Nature and Natural Resources, 1972.

"Orangutan is Dead at Fifty-Six; Zoo Lays Long Life to Diet." *New York Times.* New York: The New York Times Company, January 17, 1976.

"Orangutans, Orphans of the Wild." Television program. London: Survival Anglia Limited, April, 1976.

Poe, Edgar Allan. *Tales of Mystery and Imagination.* London: George G. Harrap & Company, Ltd., 1935.

Reynolds, Vernon. *The Apes: The Gorilla, Chimpanzee, Orangutan and Gibbon—their History and their World.* New York: E. P. Dutton & Company, Inc., 1967.

Rijksen, Herman D. "Social Structure in a Wild Orang-utan Population in Sumatra." A paper presented to the Fifth Congress of the International Primatological Society. Nagoya, Japan: August 21-25, 1974.

Rijksen, Herman D. and Rijksen-Graatsma, Ans. "Orang Utan Rescue Work in North Sumatra." *Oryx.* London: The Fauna Preservation Society, April, 1975.

Ripley, S. Dillon and the Editors of *Life. The Land and Wildlife of Tropical Asia.* New York: Life Nature Library/Time–Life Books, 1964.

Rodman, Peter S. "Population Composition and Adaptive Organisation among Orang-utans of the Kutai Reserve." *Comparative Ecology and Behaviour of Primates.* Edited by Richard P. Michael and John H. Crook. New York: Academic Press, 1973.

Rumbaugh, Duane M. and Gill, Timothy. "The Learning Skills of Great Apes." *Journal of Human Evolution,* Vol. 2. London: Academic Press, 1973.

Rumbaugh, Duane M.; Riesen, A. H. and Wright, Sue C. "Creative Responsiveness to Objects: A Report of a Pilot Study of Young Apes." *Folia Primatologica,* Vol. 17. Basel, Switzerland: S. Karger, 1972.

Sanderson, Ivan with Loth, David. *Ivan Sanderson's Book of Great Jungles.* New York: Julian Messner, 1965.

"Saving the 'Man of the Forest.'" *Time.* New York: Time Inc., July 26, 1968.

Schaller, George B. "The Orang-utan in Sarawak." *Zoologica,* Vol. 46, No. 2. New York: New York Zoological Society, 1961.

Simon, Noel and Géroudet, Paul. "Orang-utan." *Last Survivors.* New York: World Publishing Company, 1970.

"The Orang-utan." *Grzimek's Animal Life Encyclopedia.* Editor-in-Chief, Dr. C. Bernhard Grzimek. New York: Van Nostrand Reinhold Company, 1968, 1972.

"Two More Mammals." *Newsweek.* New York: Newsweek, Inc., November 3, 1975.

Wallace, Alfred Russel. *The Malay Archipelago.* New York: Harper & Brothers, 1869. (In paperback, New York: Dover Publications Inc., 1962.)

Wendt, Herbert. *From Ape to Adam: The Search for the Ancestry of Man.* New York: The Bobbs-Merrill Company, Inc., 1972.

Yerkes, Robert M. and Ada W. *The Great Apes: A Study of Anthropoid Life.* New Haven, Connecticut: Yale University Press, 1929. New York: Johnson Reprint, 1970.

Index

103 By Rod Brindamour. Copyright by the National Geographic Society.

110 Courtesy of The American Museum of Natural History.

111 From *Orang-Utan,* copyright © 1962 by Barbara Harrisson. Reprinted by permission of Doubleday & Co., Inc., and of William Collins Sons & Co., Ltd., Glascow, publishers.

113 Courtesy of Dr. Herman D. Rijksen.

121 From *Orang-Utan,* copyright © 1962 by Barbara Harrisson. Reprinted by permission of Doubleday & Co., Inc., and of William Collins Sons & Co., Ltd. Glascow, publishers.

123 From *Orang-Utan,* copyright © 1962 by Barbara Harrisson. Reprinted by permission of Doubleday & Co., Inc., and of William Collins Sons & Co., Ltd., Glascow, publishers.

125 By Carl Mydans. TIME-LIFE Picture Agency. © Time, Inc.

128 Courtesy of Dr. Herman D. Rijksen.

130 Courtesy of Dr. Herman D. Rijksen.

131 Courtesy of Dr. Herman D. Rijksen.

138 By Rod Brindamour. Copyright by the National Geographic Society.

140 By Biruté Galdikas. Copyright by the National Geographic Society.

141 By Rod Brindamour. Copyright by the National Geographic Society.

145 Gorilla by Kenneth Fink. The National Audubon Society Collection/ Photo Researchers, Inc. Others by Aline Amon.